Storage Area Networks

ISBN 0-13-027959-5

90000

9 780130 279590

Hewlett-Packard® Professional Books

OPERATING SYSTEMS

Fernandez	Configuring CDE: The Common Desktop Environment
Lund	Integrating UNIX® and PC Network Operating Systems
Madell	Disk and File Management Tasks on HP-UX
Poniatowski	HP-UX 11.x System Administration Handbook and Toolkit
Poniatowski	HP-UX 11.x System Administration "How To" Book, Second Edition
Poniatowski	HP-UX System Administration Handbook and Toolkit
Poniatowski	Learning the HP-UX Operating System
Poniatowski	UNIX® User's Handbook
Rehman	HP Certified, HP-UX System Administration
Sauers, Weygant	HP-UX Tuning and Performance
Stone, Symons	UNIX® Fault Management
Weygant	Clusters for High Availability: A Primer of HP-UX Solutions

ONLINE/INTERNET

Amor	The E-business (R)evolution
Greenberg, Lakeland	A Methodology for Developing and Deploying Internet and Intranet Solutions
Greenberg, Lakeland	Building Professional Web Sites with the Right Tools
Ketkar	Working with Netscape Server on HP-UX

NETWORKING/COMMUNICATIONS

Blommers	Practical Planning for Network Growth
Lee	The ISDN Consultant
Lucke	Designing and Implementing Computer Workgroups

ENTERPRISE

Blommers	Architecting Enterprise Solutions with UNIX® Networking
Cook	Building Enterprise Information Architectures
Pipkin	Halting the Hacker: A Practical Guide to Computer Security
Pipkin	Information Security: Protecting the Global Enterprise
Sperley	Enterprise Data Warehouse, Volume 1: Planning, Building, and Implementation
Thornburgh	Fibre Channel for Mass Storage
Thornburgh, Schoenborn	Storage Area Networks: Designing and Implementing a Mass Storage System

PROGRAMMING

Blinn	Portable Shell Programming
Caruso	Power Programming in HP OpenView
Chaudri, Loomis	Object Databases in Practice
Chew	The Java™/C++ Cross-Reference Handbook
Grady	Practical Software Metrics for Project Management and Process Improvement
Grady	Successful Software Process Improvement
Lewis	The Art & Science of Smalltalk
Lichtenbelt, Crane, Naqvi	Introduction to Volume Rendering
Mellquist	SNMP++
Mikkelsen, Pherigo	Practical Software Configuration Management
Norton, DiPasquale	Thread Time: The Multithreaded Programming Guide
Wadleigh, Crawford	Software Optimization for High Performance Computing

IMAGE PROCESSING

Crane	A Simplified Approach to Image Processing
Day	The Color Scanning Handbook
Gann	Desktop Scanners: Image Quality

OTHER TITLES OF INTEREST

Kane	PA-RISC 2.0 Architecture
Markstein	IA-64 and Elementary Functions

Storage Area Networks

Designing and Implementing a Mass Storage System

Ralph H. Thornburgh

Barry J. Schoenborn

www.hp.com/go/retailbooks

Prentice Hall PTR
Upper Saddle River, New Jersey 07458
www.phptr.com

Library of Congress Cataloging-in-Publication Data

Thornburgh, Ralph H.
    Storage area networks : designing and implementing a mass storage system/Ralph H.
Thornburgh, Barry J. Schoenborn.
            p.   cm.—(Hewlett-Packard professional books)
        Includes bibliographical references and index.
        ISBN 0-13-027959-5 (alk. paper)
        1. Computer networks. 2. Information storage and retrieval systems. 3. Computer
storage devices. I. Schoenborn, Barry J. II. Title. III. Series.

TK5105.5 .T478 2000
004.6—dc21   00-058438

Editorial/production supervision: *Jane Bonnell*   Acquisitions editor: *Jill Pisoni*
Cover design director: *Jerry Votta*   Editorial assistant: *Justin Somma*
Cover design: *Talar Agasyan*   Marketing manager: *Bryan Gambrel*
Manufacturing buyer: *Maura Zaldivar*

Manager, Hewlett-Packard Retail Book Publishing: *Patricia Pekary*
Editor, Hewlett-Packard Professional Books: *Susan Wright*

Published by Prentice Hall PTR
Prentice-Hall, Inc.
Upper Saddle River, New Jersey 07458

Prentice Hall books are widely used by corporations and government agencies for training, marketing,
and resale.
The publisher offers discounts on this book when ordered in bulk quantities. For more information,
contact Corporate Sales Department, Phone: 800-382-3419; FAX: 201-236-7141;
E-mail: corpsales@prenhall.com
Or write: Prentice Hall PTR, Corporate Sales Dept., One Lake Street, Upper Saddle River, NJ 07458.

HP and HP-UX are registered trademarks of Hewlett-Packard Company. HP-UX release 10.20 and later
and HP-UX release 11.00 and later (in both 32- and 64-bit configurations) on all HP 9000 computers
are Open Group UNIX 95 branded products. The following terms are trademarks or registered
trademarks of other companies as follows: IBM, AIX, International Business Machines Corporation;
Microsoft, Windows, Windows NT, Microsoft Corporation; DLT, DLTtape, Quantum Corporation;
Java, Solaris, Sun Microsystems, Inc.; UNIX, X/Open Company Limited. Other product or company
names mentioned herein are the trademarks or registered trademarks of their respective owners.

Printed in the United States of America
10 9 8 7 6 5 4 3 2 1

ISBN 0-13-027959-5

Prentice-Hall International (UK) Limited, *London*
Prentice-Hall of Australia Pty. Limited, *Sydney*
Prentice-Hall Canada Inc., *Toronto*
Prentice-Hall Hispanoamericana, S.A., *Mexico*
Prentice-Hall of India Private Limited, *New Delhi*
Prentice-Hall of Japan, Inc., *Tokyo*
Pearson Education Asia Pte. Ltd.
Editora Prentice-Hall do Brasil, Ltda., *Rio de Janeiro*

Contents

List of Figures

Foreword

Storage Area Networks (SANs) and the related technologies are still in their infancies and continue to evolve. SANs originated as a result of the incredible demands for storage that have developed from the digital data explosion that we are experiencing. Ralph Thornburgh and Barry Schoenborn present a very comprehensive view of today's SANs, including technologies, environments, and solutions. In an ever-changing environment such as this, they have captured both the history and the most current information about Storage Area Networks.

The SAN world today is a very complex association of hardware and software components. It is a world of very few standards, many new devices, and demands for newer and better components. This book discusses the surrounding technologies, as well as the details of what a SAN is, how it is constructed, and why one would want to implement a SAN.

You will also read about managing the SAN. SAN management software is the initial software application that will lead to many other value-added services that will add intelligence to the SAN. SAN backup and restore is also discussed. This is the initial solution that is a harbinger of myriad solutions that will begin to appear as a result of the added functionalities and capabilities that SAN architecture and SAN technologies uniquely enable.

This book is a must-read for anyone who wants to learn about or is considering adopting this technology. It has been designed in such a way as to be useful to neophytes, or as a reference book to those experienced with SANs.

Charles Trentacosti, Marketing Manager
Hewlett-Packard's Software and SAN Management Operation

Preface

Information Technology requirements change every day, but one requirement that hasn't changed since the inception of data processing is the demand for fast, reliable, and massive data storage. Economic trends in the 1990s—such as the rapid development of e-commerce, the globalization of business, and the mergers of already-giant corporations—have only escalated the demand.

Traditional data storage methods cannot keep pace with the demands placed on them. Enterprises require more information, delivered faster, and with complete reliability—and traditional methods are failing to deliver. In fact, any time the word "traditional" is used in reference to an IT methodology, there is a strong implication that the methodology is out of date.

The Storage Area Network (SAN) is the newest concept and technology for providing fast and reliable mass storage. The SAN meets today's need to store enormous amounts of data and deliver that data at tremendous speed without failure.

The SAN exhibits a flexibility for expansion and performance improvement that is typically referred to as "scalability," but that word too often limits our thinking to numbers of devices or their capacities. *How big is a disk drive? How many of them can I hook up?* Yes, a SAN is scalable in the conventional sense, but it requires an additional descriptor.

That descriptor is "modularity." In *Future Shock*, Alvin Toffler called for modularity as a method of dealing with and surviving rapid change. Individual parts of an entity have a limited lifespan, but can be changed out, so the overall entity has a longer lifespan. The Storage Area Network is highly modular, and that's one of its best features. The capabilities of SAN components are increasing even as this book is being written.

To be sure, the SAN is scalable. It can accommodate a large number of devices and store great volumes of data. Because a SAN is part hardware, part software, and part concept, it has durability and flexibility. It defies that traditional First Law of Information Technology: "As soon as you buy the product, it's obsolete."

The Storage Area Network is vital to Information Technology in the 21st century and will be with us for a long time.

What This Book Is About

This book is a comprehensive introduction to Storage Area Networks for IT professionals who must gain familiarity with this new technology.

The purpose of this book is to familiarize you with SAN technology and demonstrate its practical application in the IT environment.

You may have read an article or two about SANs, or you may have read an entire book. Chances are, however, that you have not yet encountered enough material in one publication to give you a complete SAN picture. We have found that even highly experienced system or network professionals are unfamiliar with SAN functionality and terminology.

The book opens with the basics, looking at the core definition of a SAN, a historical perspective on traditional storage (and its limitations), and the rudiments of Fibre Channel, the enabling technology for the SAN.

The middle part of the book is intended to be a comprehensive rundown of the SAN: the many ways to configure a SAN, advice on building your own SAN from your current legacy equipment, the workings of SAN backup, and managing the SAN. There's also an extensive chapter describing Hewlett-Packard SAN products.

The final portion of the book is an exercise in predicting the future. We begin with a brief interview with Duane Zitzner, President of Computing Systems at Hewlett-Packard, to provide a sense of HP's commitment to the SAN in the future.

We then anticipate how the SAN will promote dramatic changes in existing applications and will very likely create brand new applications. If technology moves at its present pace (and we have no reason to doubt that) many of our speculations will be turning into realities even as this book is published.

Who Should Read This Book

Read this book if the concept, terminology, or setup of a Storage Area Network is new to you. Whether you are an experienced IT professional or a new practitioner, you will want to make these terms and this technology part of your background.

If you are planning a new SAN, converting your present storage solution to a SAN, or building out your present SAN, you will find useful concepts and ideas in this text.

Whether you work in an all-HP shop, a non-HP shop, a heterogeneous environment, or a mainframe data center, you will still find applicable information here. We describe Hewlett-Packard hardware and software products extensively, because we are very familiar with them, and we also happen to believe they are outstanding in performance, quality and reliability.

If you fall into one of the following groups, this book should be of value to you:

- **System administrators**—those who control computer system configurations and resources

- **Network administrators**—those who configure and support networks

- **Technical support/Response center engineers**—those who support and troubleshoot mass storage resource problems for customers

- **IT executives**—those responsible for acquiring and deploying storage technology solutions

- **IT students**—those who want to get up to speed on real world business challenges

There's another person this book is intended for. That's the person who is or wants to become an IT SAN management professional. That's an individual who specializes in managing enterprise storage. The job title isn't in common use yet, but we think it will be used widely in the very near future.

By the way, it's also our intent that this book be informative, challenging, and fun for any general reader who wants to keep up with the latest technology.

How to Use This Book

Like any authors, we would be flattered if you read this book from cover to cover, from beginning to end. If you do, you'll find a planned progression from essential background information to comprehensive how-to techniques and a vision of the future. If you are unfamiliar with SANs, this is the recommended approach.

However, there are no doubt many calls on your time, and you may not be able to conveniently read all of this book. If that's the case, use it as a reference.

For example, if the development of storage doesn't interest you, or you are already familiar with the fundamentals of Fibre Channel, skip those chapters. To explore topologies or review Hewlett-Packard SAN products, go straight to those chapters.

If you are in a very great hurry, read the compact summary below.

Chapter 1: The Storage Area Network. We introduce and define the SAN, establish its value, and describe its component technologies.

Chapter 2: A Brief History of Storage. This chapter contains a chronology of storage, from the Big Bang (actually, a little later) up to today's non-SAN solutions. There is value in seeing the progression of storage innovations that brought us to the SAN.

Chapter 3: A Brief Review of Fibre Channel. Fibre Channel is the enabling technology of the SAN. SANs won't work without it. This chapter explains the significant concepts, presented in as compact a form as possible.

Chapter 4: The SAN in Detail. This chapter explores an extensive array of device and connectivity options, and brings out the advantages and disadvantages of each.

Chapter 5: Managing the SAN. The best SAN is a well-managed SAN. This chapter describes HP management and monitoring software for devices and SANs.

Chapter 6: Backup and Restore. Despite the reliability of a SAN, you still need to plan for backups and restores, offsite storage, and disaster recovery scenarios (when in doubt, make a copy). This chapter covers those topics.

Chapter 7: Industry Implementations. The SAN is not a theoretical construct; it exists in many business sectors and can dramatically increase efficiency. You'll also see that some SAN-based data management techniques, such as backup or disaster recovery, cross all major industry sectors.

Chapter 8: Hewlett-Packard SAN Products. This chapter catalogs the principal SAN products available from Hewlett-Packard and shows how they can be implemented in your SAN.

Chapter 9: An Interview with Duane Zitzner. We ask a senior HP executive to describe HP's positioning and commitment to SAN technology in times to come.

Chapter 10: Future Developments. We look to the future, exploring emerging applications that will use SANs. We offer a final word about SANs.

Glossary. A glossary can be one of the most useful parts of a book. We have included a wealth of SAN and Fibre Channel terms.

Acknowledgments

We have many people to thank for their contributions to our book. A number of them are instrumental in developing Storage Area Network products at Hewlett-Packard Company. Others, from HP and beyond, have provided information essential to the book's content. A third group has given us valuable suggestions for improving the readability of the book and access to its content.

The subject of SANs is already enormous. With each new addition or variation in technology and products, the variables in SAN implementation grow exponentially. Changes occur every day. Although we are grateful to the many contributors of source information for this book, we are solely responsible for any errors or omissions.

We'd especially like to acknowledge the following people:

Eddie Alabastro, Hewlett-Packard, Roseville, CA. We thank him for his technical review of this material.

Christian Bauman, copy editor for Prentice Hall Professional Technical Reference. Chris found many errors we thought couldn't possibly be there.

Kyle Black, Solutions Consulting Manager, Hewlett-Packard Storage Organization, Roseville, CA. Kyle reviewed the book for technical accuracy, pointed out our errors and omissions, and made suggestions for improvement.

Jane Bonnell, Production Editor at Prentice Hall Professional Technical Reference. She was always helpful and encouraging during the final phases of production. She also made us turn things in on time.

David F. Clark, Technical Writer, Willow Valley Software, Nevada City, CA. He edited text, repaired graphics, added index entries, and provided highly useful ideas and comments.

Jennifer Harrington, Manager, Integration Testing and Training Team, Business Process Information Engineering Section, North American Business PCs, Hewlett-Packard, Roseville, CA. She was this book's champion (and is also Ralph's manager).

Victor Hendrickse, Hewlett-Packard, Roseville, CA. We thank him for his technical review of this material.

Mary Hynes, R&D Lab Manager, Software and SAN Management Operation (SSMO), Hewlett-Packard, Roseville, CA. She is our book's sponsor.

Jill Pisoni, Executive Editor, Prentice Hall Professional Technical Reference, Upper Saddle River, NJ. She guided the entire effort.

Charles F. Trentacosti, Marketing Manager, Software and SAN Management Operation, Hewlett-Packard, Roseville, CA. Charlie wrote the Foreword to this book.

Kathleen Williams, occasional subcontractor with Willow Valley Software and now employed at Unify Corporation, Sacramento, CA. She was a significant developer of the last release of the HP SureStore E Disk Array XP256 documentation. We thank her for diligent efforts and sense of humor in pointing out the flaws in our work.

Susan Wright, Editorial Director, Hewlett-Packard Professional Books. She kept us on track during the whole development process.

Duane E. Zitzner, President of Hewlett-Packard Company's Computing Systems. He was able to take time from his busy schedule to share his vision of SANs and their place in HP's future.

About the Authors

RALPH THORNBURGH

Ralph Thornburgh has worked for Hewlett-Packard Company for 25 years as an IT trainer, IT Data Center Manager, and Learning Products Engineer (technical writer).

He worked in Information Systems for 13 years (as a trainer for three years and a Data Center Manager for 10 years). For the last 11 years he was a Learning Products Engineer. He is currently a Training Engineering Consultant for the Integration Testing and Training Team, Business Process Information Engineering Section, Business PCs North America, at Hewlett-Packard in Roseville, CA.

During this time he created 24 classes for Hewlett-Packard data center employees and support personnel worldwide. He has also written numerous user manuals and technical support manuals.

He led the team that wrote the multicourse training program for Hewlett-Packard's implementation of Fibre Channel for Mass Storage and two classes for other Hewlett-Packard Fibre Channel peripheral devices.

Recently, he led the team that wrote the documentation set for HP's newest mass storage device, the SureStore E Disk Array XP256, containing one familiarization guide and seven user guides for the product's monitoring and management software.

Ralph held a secondary teaching certificate for three years. He designed and delivered computer class curricula—including courses on operating systems and computer operations—for The Computer Learning Center in Santa Clara,

CA. He also designed, developed, and delivered an American Sign Language (ASL) course for middle-school children.

Ralph was in the U.S. Army for eleven years and is a Vietnam veteran. He spent time in the California Army National Guard as a section training sergeant, training soldiers in technical skills, such as aviation electronics, and basic combat skills, such as land navigation (map reading) and basic marksmanship.

Ralph is the author of *Fibre Channel for Mass Storage*, a book about the fundamentals of Fibre Channel and Hewlett-Packard's Fibre Channel products.

BARRY SCHOENBORN

Barry Schoenborn is an independent technical writer with over 29 years experience creating documentation for computer hardware and software. He owns Willow Valley Software, a technical documentation company located in Nevada City, California.

He has provided documentation services to Hewlett-Packard Company for the last seven years. He has documented Fibre Channel host bus adapters for the System Interconnect Solutions Lab in Cupertino, network appliances for the Network Peripheral Solutions Division in Roseville, tape devices for HP's Worldwide Technology Expert Center in Texas, and mass storage for the Enterprise Storage Business Unit in Roseville.

Barry has written dozens of user and service manuals for HP devices and software. Recently, he worked on the team that wrote HP's Fibre Channel for Mass Storage training and the documentation set for HP's newest and largest mass storage device, the SureStore E Disk Array XP256.

He has owned his own company for 17 years. In addition to HP, clients have included The Money Store, Mitsubishi, and Delta Dental Plan of California. Prior to that, he worked for Xerox Corporation, McDonnell Douglas, Aratex, and Beneficial Standard Life Insurance Company. He has worked as a programmer, computer operator, and EDP auditor.

Barry also operates Willow Valley Press, which publishes the works of local authors. He writes a monthly political column for *The Union* newspaper of Grass Valley/Nevada City, and makes frequent appearances on the Nevada County News Hour on community access television.

CHAPTER 1

The Storage Area Network

This chapter discusses:

- **What is a SAN?**
- **Why are SANs needed?**
- **The signs of a SAN**

We introduce and define the SAN, establish its value, and describe the underlying technologies.

1.1 What Is a SAN?

Every book you will ever read about Storage Area Networks will start with this question. There is no one simple answer, but there are multiple simple answers (and they don't conflict with each other).

- A SAN is a mass storage solution, designed to provide enormous amounts of mass storage to an enterprise. It is fast, reliable, and highly scalable.

- According to Transoft Networks of Santa Barbara, California (recently acquired by Hewlett-Packard), the SAN is the next generation high-speed network architecture.

- According to Clariion, in a 1999 presentation by Ken Kutzer, Storage Area Networks Product Marketing Manager, a SAN is a "Network infra-structure that connects computers and devices, transports device com-mands, and runs value-added software."

- A SAN is identified by special connection architecture, known as Fibre Channel. Fibre Channel is (in the words of Dave Simpson, Editor-in-Chief of *INFOSTOR*) "the key enabling technology behind SANs."

- A SAN is identified by one or more (usually more) servers connected to an infinitely variable number and arrangement of storage devices, by means of Fibre Channel hubs, switches, and bridges.

- A SAN is identified by its components, usually high capacity, highly redundant (and therefore failure-resistant) storage devices.

- A SAN is a topology with three distinct features: 1) storage is not directly connected to network clients, 2) storage is not directly con-nected to the servers, and 3) the storage devices are interconnected.

Every manufacturer of computer hardware or software intended for Storage Area Networks has similar definitions.

If you read no further in this book, at least take a look at Figure 1-1. It shows a SAN and its common components.

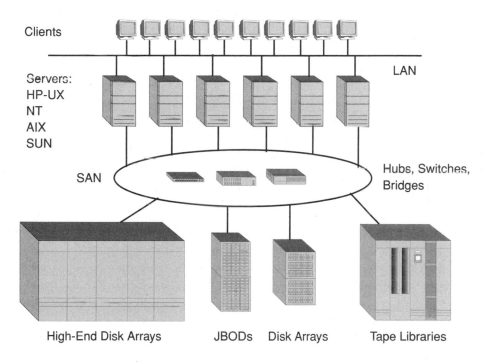

Figure 1-1 A Storage Area Network

No server is connected to any one storage device, and all storage devices are potentially available to all servers. Connections between devices are made using hubs, switches, and bridges.

The SAN pictured is an ideal SAN, with a variety of storage devices, interconnection devices, and servers. The "loop" in the illustration is intended only to suggest the interconnection of the devices; it isn't an actual connection scheme.

1.1.1 What a SAN Is Not

A SAN is not embedded storage. *Embedded storage* is not SAN storage. No matter how many disk drives there are, how large the capacity of the drives, or how many servers are attached to the LAN, it's still not a SAN. The disk drives are resident in the server.

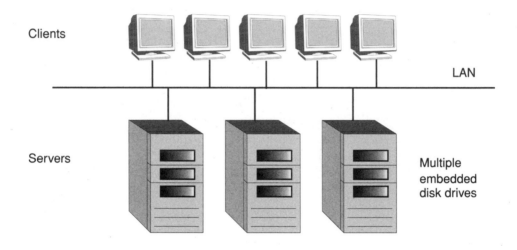

Figure 1-2 Embedded Storage

In Figure 1-2, the amount of storage is limited by the server's capacity to accommodate it.

For smaller operations, there's nothing wrong with filling the server's drive bay with high-capacity drives, but there is a physical limit. Also, the arrangement amounts to putting all your eggs in one basket, and a server failure would make a great deal of data unavailable.

As you will see later, SANs are scalable. In theory, thousands of devices may be added to a SAN. In practice, SAN scalability is limited by performance issues and the current physical capabilities of hubs and switches.

A SAN is not directly attached storage. *Directly attached storage* (as shown in Figure 1-3) is a simple extension of embedded storage, with one or more JBODs (Just a Bunch of Disks) or disk arrays connected by SCSI directly to (and typically only to) one server.

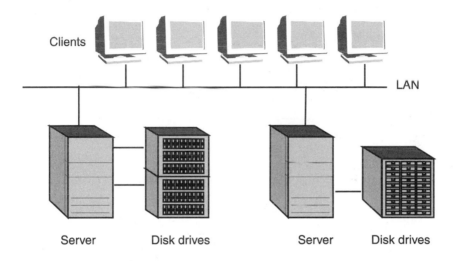

Figure 1-3 Directly Attached Storage

No matter how many arrays there are, or the capacity of the drives, it's still not a SAN.

The scalability of directly attached SCSI-based storage is ultimately limited by the number of SCSI bus adapters and addresses available to the server.

Sharing SCSI-based storage between servers takes place over the LAN. This produces a performance penalty for the client workstations on the LAN. The clients need speedy server access, but in this arrangement, they must share LAN bandwidth with servers requesting data from other servers' disk storage.

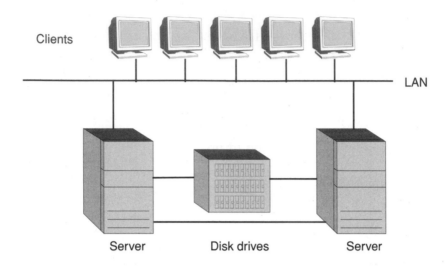

Clients

LAN

Server   Disk drives   Server

Figure 1-4   Directly Attached Shared Storage

What about sharing storage directly between servers? Figure 1-4 shows a cluster of two servers sharing disk drives without moving disk I/O over the LAN. However, this configuration cannot readily be expanded to include additional servers. The scalability of directly attached storage, shared or nonshared, is limited.

A SAN is not Network Attached Storage.   Network Attached Storage is highly useful in many business operations. It's amazingly easy to bring additional storage onto the LAN, and some manufacturers advertise it as a three step process—plug in the RJ-45 network cable, plug in the power, and turn the storage device on. That's not too far from the truth. In addition, the products often feature RAID technology for data redundancy and a tape drive for backup.

Well and good, but it's not a SAN. Storage is scalable, and data is highly redundant, but attaching storage devices to a LAN can degrade the performance of all processing. While NAS works fine in small and medium operations, in larger operations the performance math will eventually catch up to it.

Client access to data requires client-server and server-NAS interaction. A client request for a record means that: 1) the client requests the record over the LAN; 2) the server requests the record from NAS over the LAN; 3) the NAS device serves up the record over the LAN; and 4) the server delivers the record to the client over the LAN.

Because both client access and storage access interactions use the LAN, there is a quick buildup in traffic and "traffic penalties" on the LAN. The mathematics will vary depending on the kind of processing, but in general terms each new client adds a small traffic burden (its own I/Os) to the LAN, and each new NAS device adds a large traffic burden (everybody's I/Os) to the LAN.

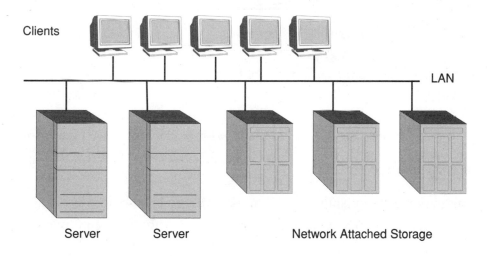

Figure 1-5   Network Attached Storage (NAS)

Network Attached Storage (NAS) lives "in front of the server" (see Figure 1-5). In his book, *Designing Storage Area Networks*, Tom Clark accurately describes the SAN as being located "behind the server."

That's an important contrast. The SAN puts storage where I/Os don't impact the clients. The significant contribution of NAS is the idea of networking storage devices. However, it takes a SAN to put the storage behind the server.

1.1.2 What a SAN Is

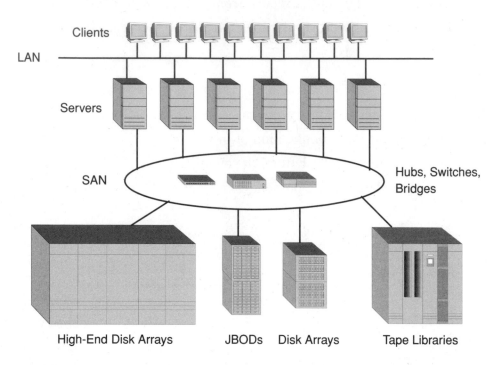

Figure 1-6 Storage Behind the Server

The major distinguishing marks of a SAN are: 1) storage lives behind the servers, not on the LAN, and 2) multiple servers can share multiple storage devices.

In Figure 1-6, the LAN is the traditional connection topology, referred to by Xerox and other early LAN innovators as "bus" topology. However, the storage devices are not on the LAN bus. They have their own independent connection scheme—a Storage Area Network. It is shown as a loop to suggest that the storage devices are connected together, although the devices are not always connected in a loop. Multiple pools of connected devices are possible as well.

The interconnected group of mass storage includes high-end disk arrays, mid-range disk arrays, JBODs, tape libraries, and optical storage devices. The devices are accessible to all servers through hubs, switches and bridges.

There is client-server interaction over the LAN and server-storage interaction over the SAN. Neither group of devices needs to share bandwidth with the other.

Notice that more than one server participates in the SAN storage pool. The number of servers is limited only by the physical capabilities of the connecting devices. The same is true of the number of storage devices that can be attached.

1.1.3 SAN Servers

There has been a predictable and understandable pattern in the evolution of client-server configurations. With a single server, you'd begin by running applications and storing data for those applications on embedded disk drives. As storage requirements grew, you'd add attached storage. Eventually, there would be a need for another server, which would likely run different applications and access its own data stored on the second server.

That simple model didn't last long, and for these reasons:

1. The storage requirements of different applications grow at different rates. Despite the best planning efforts, it's hard to avoid server configurations where one server has disk space to burn and another is hurting for space.

2. Comprehensive databases contain a lot of data to be shared. The highly integrated, highly shareable database is one of the Holy Grails of Information Technology. However, because of size and the value of the data to multiple applications, a big database is better being placed on an external storage device than on a server.

3. Servers can fail, so it's not a smart idea to risk data becoming unavailable by placing it on only one server.

The point is that a SAN pools the data and offers relatively easy access to the data by multiple servers. This lessens the dependence on any one server. The possibility of a truly durable, failure-proof information system begins to emerge.

Further, it's very easy to add more storage, and it's immediately accessible by all servers. For that matter, it's very easy to add more servers.

In an enterprise containing servers with a common operating system type, such as HP-UX, connectivity from any server to any storage device attached to the SAN is relatively easy. This is a homogeneous server environment.

But what about mixed servers, from different manufacturers, with different operating systems? With the right equipment and a good design, a SAN can support heterogeneous servers. This can be a combination of HP-UX servers, Windows NT servers, and other open system (UNIX) servers. HP places its emphasis on HP-UX, Windows NT, AIX, Sun Solaris, and Linux.

Other manufacturers have the same concerns about heterogeneous server environments. Also, Hewlett-Packard has announced its commitment to an open SAN architecture.

Mixing heterogeneous equipment is a "real-world" problem, because some IT departments have acquired quite a mix of servers. The goal of a heterogeneous-server SAN is to share data between servers running different operating systems.

Data sharing is possible to the extent that different operating systems can understand and use each others' file systems. This promise is not yet fulfilled, since Windows NT, UNIX, and IBM mainframe file systems are intolerant of each other. In time, however, data is likely to be shared with greater ease.

If data can't be shared directly, it can be converted. For example, Hitachi, IBM, and HP have software for "mainframe-to-open" and "open-to-mainframe" data conversions. This software typically operates on disk arrays that can emulate both IBM volumes and open system logical units (LUNs).

However, even if servers don't share (or can't convert) different data types stored on a SAN, there are still equipment cost and management benefits in sharing different disks on the same physical device.

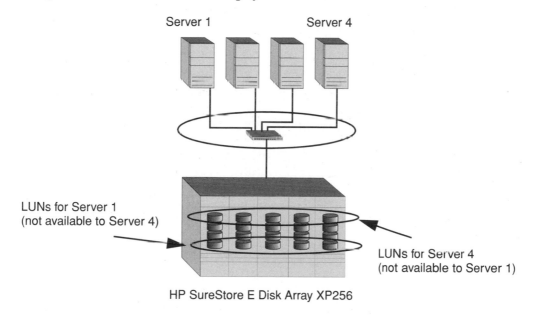

Figure 1-7   Sharing a Physical Device, But Not Sharing LUNs

With appropriate software (such as HP's Secure LUN feature used with the XP256 disk array) servers can "own" their share of disks (actually, logical units, or LUNs) on the same storage device (Figure 1-7). In fact, quite the opposite from sharing data, LUNs can be "zoned" to prevent interactions with unauthorized servers.

1.1.4 SAN Storage Devices

A distinguishing mark of the Storage Area Network is the wealth of storage devices that can be attached to the SAN.

The number of devices that can be connected is limited by the theoretical and practical limits of the hubs, switches, and bridges that interconnect servers with storage devices. As you will see, the theoretical limits are quite large, while the practical limits are a bit tamer.

Any disk device can contain numerous disk mechanisms ("mechs"). The HP FC30 has 30 disk drives, the HP FC60 has 60 drives, and the XP256 has up to 256 drives.

Any SAN-ready storage device can participate in the SAN storage pool with minimum difficulty, because no matter what its purpose (high-availability disk storage, plain old disk storage, near-line optical storage, tape storage), it will be identified by address to the servers that interact with it.

A SAN-ready device is a Fibre Channel device. SCSI devices (primarily legacy devices, but also the most current tape libraries) can participate in the SAN by means of Fibre Channel/SCSI bridges (Figure 1-8).

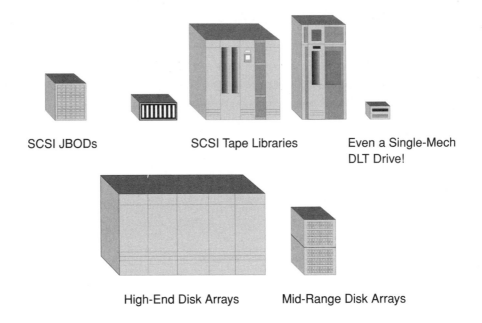

SCSI JBODs   SCSI Tape Libraries   Even a Single-Mech
                                                      DLT Drive!

High-End Disk Arrays   Mid-Range Disk Arrays

Figure 1-8 SAN Storage Devices

Disk Arrays. The high-end, high-performance, highly managed disk array typifies the direction in which SAN storage devices are going. The Hewlett-Packard SureStore E Disk Array XP256 is a good example. It stores over 12 terabytes (TB) of data, using a maximum of 256 47 GB disks, and disk capacity points seem to be rising every day. Also, as this book goes to press, HP has announced the introduction of the XP512 disk array.

Large IT operations are by no means limited to single large disk array. A bank or insurance company data center might run eight of these giant devices on a single SAN.

A high-end disk array is fast and highly redundant, with multiple fans, power supplies, and controllers. It also supports multiple paths to the SAN, eliminating a single point of failure.

The XP256 is "self-healing" to the extent that a number of components can fail, yet the device will keep on functioning. When something goes wrong, the disk array calls the Hewlett-Packard response center to report a need for service.

There are many other disk arrays, so you can find SAN-ready equipment that's sized exactly right and has sufficient redundancy for your operation.

SCSI JBODs. SCSI JBODs can be connected to a SAN through Fibre Channel/SCSI bridges. Even a single-spindle mechanism ("mech") can be a citizen on the SAN, although this is rarely seen. Non-HA (high availability) devices can be useful components on a SAN.

However, judging from business trends, we would expect the high-capacity, high-availability disk array to dominate disk storage over the next several years.

The business trends are e-business, rapid expansion, global consolidation, and round-the-clock operation. SAN-attached storage devices will answer the needs by serving up mountains of data and providing failure-proof delivery of information to the enterprise.

Tape Libraries. Tape libraries of virtually any scale can and should be part of a SAN. Your installation may be a single large tape library (using DLT or one of the new formats we'll discuss later), or require multiple DLT tape libraries. In fact, in a recent issue of *INFOSTOR*, it was reported that one data center had a need for speedy multiple copies of tape backups. Multiple DLT tape libraries accomplished this, filling the need and producing a new acronym, RAIL. RAIL stands for "Random Array of Independent Libraries."

A SAN can permit communication directly between storage devices. with minimum server interaction. This means that direct disk-to-disk and disk-to-tape backups are possible. This permits concepts such as "LAN-less" and "server-less" backup.

1.1.5 SAN Connection Medium

The connection technology for a SAN is Fibre Channel. As will be shown in greater detail in Chapter 3, Fibre Channel's distinguishing marks are speed and distance.

Speed.   Fibre Channel currently moves data at "gigabit speed"; that is 1 Gbps, or 1063 Mbps (some sources cite 1063.5 Mbps or 1064 Mbps). That's approximately 100 megabytes per second. According to *INFOSTOR*, a number of vendors have demonstrated 2 Gbps Fibre Channel, and 4 Gbps Fibre Channel technology is planned for the future. This evolution clearly puts Ultra SCSI in second place as a speedy medium.

When you see a proliferation of thin orange (typically) fiber cables in a data center, starting to crowd out SCSI cables, it is certain that you're in a Fibre Channel shop and chances are good that you are in a SAN shop.

What can be a little confusing is that Fibre Channel data transport is supported over both fiber cable and copper. However, copper is seen mainly in intra-cabinet connections between devices, and fiber cable is used far more widely.

Fiber Channel can be used for terminal-server interconnects, running at "quarter speed," or 266 Mbps, but we've not seen any proliferation of Fibre Channel for this purpose. The main purpose of Fibre Channel is to connect mass storage devices and servers over a SAN.

Distance.   Fibre Channel can connect devices over relatively long distances. For now, take it as a general rule that there may be a distance of up to 500 meters between a device and a hub, and up to 10 km between hubs.

Fibre Channel's ability to span distances makes SCSI, with its 25-meter distance limitation, a noncompetitor when it comes to moving data through a building or across a campus.

ATM.   Asynchronous Transfer Mode (ATM) connections can appear in a SAN. This connectivity option will move data from site to site over distances of thousands of kilometers.

SCSI.   SCSI connections appear in a SAN when a device does not have Fibre Channel capability. They can be connected to FC/SCSI bridges, and the bridges are connected to the SAN with fiber cable.

1.1.6 SAN Interconnection Devices

SAN interconnection devices are hubs, switches, bridges, and Fibre Channel host bus adapters (Figure 1-9). You'll learn more about the details of their operation in Chapters 3 and 4.

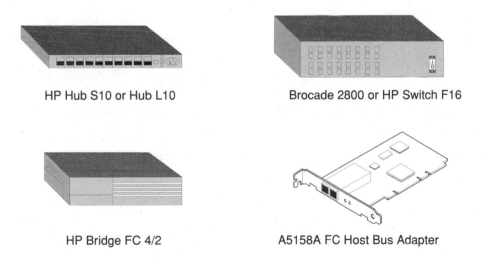

HP Hub S10 or Hub L10   Brocade 2800 or HP Switch F16

HP Bridge FC 4/2   A5158A FC Host Bus Adapter

Figure 1-9   SAN Interconnect Devices

Hubs.   Fibre Channel Arbitrated Loop (FC-AL) hubs are widely used to form the SAN, and there are cascading options to increase distances between devices and the number of ports available for connecting devices.

Although in theory up to 126 devices can participate in an FC-AL loop, as a practical matter the number of devices deployed on a hub will be limited. One limitation is the number of ports (10 on a typical hub, 18 when two hubs are cascaded). Another limitation is a decline in performance when too many devices contend for bandwidth in a loop (which is a shared, polling environment).

Switches.   Fabric switches are gaining prominence, and are now replacing hubs in some implementations.

In theory, a switch allows over 16 million simultaneous connections (based on address) to the SAN. However, a typical switch will have fewer than 16 million ports. The Brocade 2800 fabric switch and the HP Switch F16 each have 16 ports, and there are cascading options.

At this time, even though a switch typically costs about four times as much as a hub, the performance of switches makes them the better interconnection device.

Bridges.   The Fibre Channel bridge (for example the HP SureStore E Bridge FC 4/2) is essential for bringing SCSI equipment onto the SAN. The bridge is used to connect legacy or specialized SCSI equipment to the SAN. In addition, since virtually no tape libraries offered at this time are SAN-ready, the use of bridges on the SAN is essential for tape backup.

Host Bus Adapters.   Fibre Channel host bus adapters live in the servers, and provide the connection to the SAN's hubs and switches. They come with HSC or PCI interfaces, single or double ports, and replaceable Gigabit Link Modules (GLMs) or Gigabit Interface Controllers (GBICs). Fibre Channel HBAs are usually based on Agilent Technologies' Tachyon or TachLite chip.

1.1.7 SAN Distances

SAN components may be located close to or relatively far away from servers. Typically, a SAN would have most or all of its storage devices in one room or in separate rooms on one floor of a building. The LAN connects workstations in different departments to the servers.

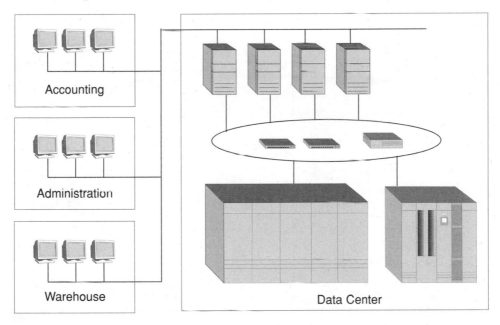

Figure 1-10   An In-building SAN

The arrangement shown in Figure 1-10 is the same as most non-SAN data centers, and exhibits the same advantages: security, ease of management, and straightforward migration from SCSI to Fibre Channel.

Tape storage may be in a different room than disk storage or servers. The data center may be on a different floor of the building from other departments. Using even the relatively short distances available with short wave hubs (500 meters), there are many data center configuration options.

In some enterprises, "local" means "on the same campus"; in others, it means across town. Perhaps the servers are located in different buildings, but they are connected to the same SAN (Figure 1-11).

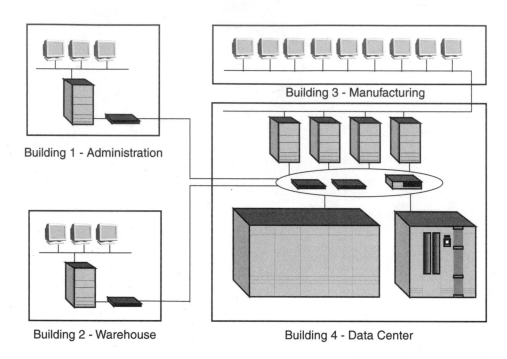

Building 1 - Administration

Building 3 - Manufacturing

Building 2 - Warehouse

Building 4 - Data Center

Figure 1-11   An On-campus or Crosstown SAN

Fibre Channel longwave hubs readily provide for connection distances of up to 10 km, so distance should not pose a problem. Many large corporations have campuses resembling small towns, and have worked through the engineering challenges of providing telephone and LAN connections between buildings. For crosstown connections, there are a number of leased-line options available.

   The cross-country SAN (Figure 1-12) is accomplished by using additional Wide Area Network (WAN) hardware. Leased lines range in speed from up to 1.544 Mbps for T-1 to up to 622 Mbps for OC-12.

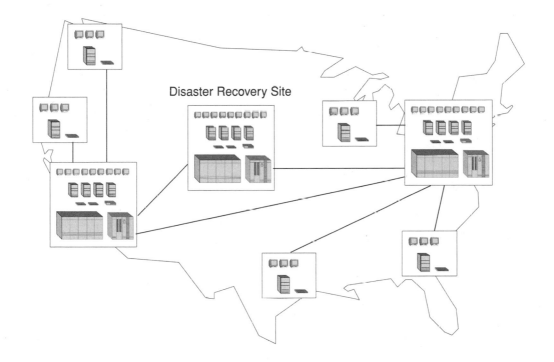

Figure 1-12   A Cross-country SAN

   The cross-country SAN is not only possible, but sometimes essential. For example, a company in earthquake-prone Los Angeles may find it prudent to mirror its data in Arizona or Nevada.

   In addition, there are cost saving advantages in centralizing data in regional or national data centers. It takes fewer administrators to manage large amounts of data, maintain equipment, expand capabilities, and protect data.

   Companies with offices worldwide can follow the cross-country model. They will need to design SANs to store data that must be both centralized and distributed.

1.2 Why Are SANs Needed?

Virtually every sector of commerce has an immense requirement for capacity, speed, and reliability in storing data. Government and education, although restrained by budget considerations, have the same requirement. And every enterprise is concerned with managing storage costs.

Capacity. In traditional business applications, simple growth of customer and manufacturing data drives the need for capacity. Business consolidations and worldwide commerce also drive the need. More data means more disk drives, greater capacity drives, and more densely populated enclosures to hold them.

New approaches to running traditional businesses drive a demand for storage. For example, data warehousing and data mining are methodologies that are producing gains for the businesses that use them. These are data-hungry constructs. In fact, at least one authority suggests that the warehouse and the data mine best serve the business as separate entities. That could amount to an instant doubling of storage requirements, and data warehouses typically aren't small.

In newer businesses, applications seem to need intense capacity and speed from their inception. Judging by the financial news, almost any e-commerce activity will ramp up from conception to reality in just months (possibly weeks), and some have become instant successes. Online retail sales, online business-to-business sales, and online auctions can attract millions of customers practically overnight. E-commerce is dramatic in its hunger for capacity, speed, and reliability in storage.

Video production, video-on-demand, and other imaging applications have storage requirements that make buying a book online look like child's play. It's fair to say that much wanted or much needed applications will not come into existence without the SAN.

Conventional storage methods can no longer satisfy the capacity requirements of mass storage. The scale of computing and the complexity of applications drive the demand for Storage Area Networks.

Reliability. In all business sectors, the cost of downtime is larger than ever. In a presentation by Computer Network Technology at HP World '99, the costs of downtime were cited (shown in Table 1-1). The source is the Fibre Channel Industry Association.

Table 1-1 The Cost of Downtime

Business	Hourly Downtime Cost
Brokerage	$6,450,000
Credit card sales authorization	$2,600,000
Pay per view	$150,000
Home shopping	$113,000
Catalog sales	$90,000
Airline reservations	$90,000
Teleticket sales	$69,000
Package shipping	$28,000
ATMs	$14,500

A SAN is Information Technology's best answer to avoiding downtime catastrophes, whether the "catastrophe" amounts to an hour less of selling books, or a week of nonoperation due to a major hurricane. A SAN lends itself to disaster recovery scenarios better than previous storage strategies.

Costs. In all business sectors, reduction of IT operating costs is all too often a dominant factor in driving IT choices. Business is always interested in a lower price per gigabyte for mass storage, and the hardware manufacturers are accommodating them. Business is also interested in lowering the labor costs for maintenance, management, and expansion, which can be intensive. Fortunately for IT management, a Storage Area Network can be maintained, managed, and expanded with relative ease by fewer people than required by non-SAN sites. There will still be $90,000-a-year system administrators, but there will be fewer of them at a single site.

1.3 The Signs of a SAN

In summary, a SAN is a combination of hardware devices, interconnect strategy, and concept. Even as the capabilities of the hardware and speed of the interconnect change, the concept will remain stable.

A collection of servers, mass storage, interconnect devices, and interconnection media constitutes a Storage Area Network, if it exhibits most of the following characteristics:

- Storage is behind the server

- Storage devices are connected to each other

- Multiple servers are connected to the storage pool

- Heterogeneous servers may be connected to the storage pool

- Fibre Channel connectivity (fiber optic cable and FC host bus adapters) is used

- Fibre Channel hubs and switches are present

- Multiple paths to devices exist

CHAPTER 2

A Brief History of Storage

This chapter discusses:

- **How did we get to networking storage anyway?**
- **Tapes**
- **Disks**
- **Local Area Networks (LANs)**
- **Network Attached Storage (NAS)**
- **RAID**
- **Mass storage**
- **Storage Area Networks**

Data storage has evolved over decades. This historical perspective shows how storage "grew up."

2.1 How Did We Get to Networking Storage Anyway?

Remember your very first computer class where the teacher talked about the three basic elements of a computer (Figure 2-1)?

INPUT ⟶ **PROCESSING** ⟶ **OUTPUT**

Figure 2-1   Basic Elements of a Computer

Then the teacher said there were three functions to the processing element. That processing consisted of the:

- control function
- arithmetic logic unit (ALU)
- memory

This is where it all began—with the core memory, the internal storage. It was also called "short-term storage." This short-term storage, also known as "volatile storage," was used by a program during the processing of instructions, and then it was made available for the next program to use.

One of us (Barry) has an early memory of such processing:

At the risk of sounding like I grew up with mastodons, I remember the early 1960s, when my high school math class was taken to Control Data Corporation in Sacramento, CA, to do some programming. At the console keyboard (electric typewriter, really), each of us took a turn entering numeric op codes and physical addresses from hand-written notes. It was a thrill to watch the program run. Of course, when my turn was done, my program was cleared out so the next one could be entered.

Long-term storage was simply the paper the report was printed on. All the data from the program had to be printed out because there was no place else to store it.

As you may know, paper tape was once a fashionable place to store the program, and data too. After all, it had respectable roots with the Teletype machine as a medium for pre-coding and duplicating messages. Further, it did not go out of fashion as long ago as people may think. In 1984, for example, as PCs were making their appearance in business, paper tape was still the medium of choice for entering APT (Automatic Programmed Tools) instructions into CAD/CAM machine tools.

A significant storage medium was the punch card, or Hollerith card (eventually known universally as the "IBM card," to the dismay of Burroughs and Univac). Cards had been storing data since the 1890 census. In 1911, Charles Flint effected the merger of Hollerith's Tabulating Machine Co. with the Computing Scale Co. of America and the International Time Recording Co., giving us C-T-R, which was to become IBM.

For decades, data stored on cards was processed on tabulating ("tab") equipment, not computers. When technology evolved to a point where there was such a thing as a stored program computer, cards could be used to store programs, input data, or output data.

As technology developed, long-term, external storage became available in the form of magnetic tapes and disks. However, the "keypunch department" was still an important part of the data center as late as the late 1970s.

2.2 Tapes

Tape was an alternate long-term storage medium whereby the data created by a program could be stored for reuse by the same program or by other programs requiring the same data.

This was the golden age of sequential processing. For example, consider a program that ran daily to maintain customer information on a master customer list. The customer master file was kept on tape, and when the update program called for it, the tape was mounted on a tape drive—a read/write device the size of a refrigerator. The day's changes (adds, changes, and deletes) might be on cards (the transaction deck) or tape (the transaction tape). When the program ran, new customers would be added, old customers deleted, and existing customer information changed as needed.

Each record on the master file would be read from the tape, put into internal memory, modified as needed and then rewritten to a new tape mounted on another tape drive (the updated master, which would be used the next day). (See Figure 2-2.)

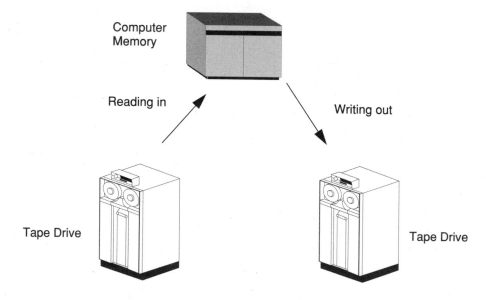

Figure 2-2   Tape Usage

Every record on the master was read and rewritten, whether it was to be changed or not.

Tapes started out 1/2-inch wide and approximately 600 feet long, with a density of 800 bytes per inch (bpi). This was great at the time, certainly a great improvement over carrying around trays of punch cards. However, as processing requirements grew there was an increased need for more storage capacity. Therefore the tapes were increased in length from 600 to 1200 feet. About the same time, the density doubled from 800 bpi to 1600 bpi.

Then, to answer the demand for increased storage, the tape length was increased again to 2400 feet and the density was increased to 6250 bpi. Notice that "the demand for increased storage" is becoming a persistent theme in data processing.

The tape reel size didn't change from the 1200 foot to the 2400 foot reel. The length of tape was simply doubled, as shown in Figure 2-3.

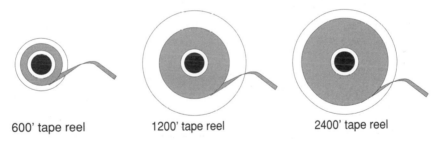

600' tape reel   1200' tape reel   2400' tape reel

Figure 2-3   Tape Capacity Growth

Tape, of course, is a sequential storage medium. *Sequential* meaning one right after the other. This makes tape a fine candidate for long-term storage, but certainly limited in terms of the speed of data retrieval.

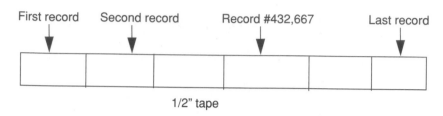

Figure 2-4   Sequential Data

When a specific record must be read, and that record is near the end of the reel, then the tape must move through all preceding data to get to the required data (Figure 2-4). Tapes are still with us, and so is this limitation.

Even though tapes were considered fast at the time, it still took too much time to access and read tape data. This is where disks came in.

2.3 Disks

Disks are called direct access storage devices (DASD). Although they can store sequential data just like tape, their claim to fame has always been direct access.

Records can be written anywhere on a disk and can be accessed directly from their disk location. There's no need to read hundreds or thousands of preceding data blocks. That means disk access is fast.

By the way, mainframe manufacturers experimented with drums and data cells as direct access storage methodologies, but they never gained any acceptance to speak of.

Disks drives weren't cheap, and a small mainframe shop might have four drives, each the size of a washing machine. By contrast, the shop might have eight tape drives. The disk drives were too expensive to hold data permanently, so the disk platters were mounted in removable, interchangeable disk packs. These looked a lot like blue plastic garbage can lids. Even though capacity was limited, access to the data was much faster because of the direct access method of data retrieval.

There were two things that governed DASD access speed:

1. The speed of rotation of the disks (referred to as latency)

2. The speed of movement of the access arms for the read/write heads (referred to as seek time)

The faster these two speeds, the faster data could be retrieved from a disk. For a while this became a static and accepted speed. No one was working on making these two speeds any faster. (Well, IBM 3330 drives were replaced with 3340s and 3344s, but we no longer have the slightest memory of what improvements these numbers represent.) And in a world of batch processing and highly segregated applications, this setup worked pretty well.

However, because databases began to grow larger and larger, the demand for more and faster storage devices grew. Interactive computing with terminals became the norm, and batch processing began to go the way of the dodo, the passenger pigeon, and the keypunch supervisor.

At the same time, computers were coming down in size and the large mainframe computer wasn't the only choice any longer. Small and midrange computer systems ("minicomputers") were becoming more prolific. The smaller computers were also becoming just as fast as the mainframes.

The great-great-grandfather of the server may have been IBM's 3790. This mid-1970s machine—the size of a deepfreeze—not only had a local database, but could actually transmit a copy of daily transaction data to a central site to keep a centralized database current. The cabinet contained exactly one large, permanent, vertically hung disk platter (about 30" in diameter), offering the immense storage capacity of 10 MB. Optionally, you could build it out to 20 MB or 30 MB by hanging additional platters.

In the 1980s the Small Computer System Interface (SCSI) protocol and connectivity was developed and became very popular. It gave the smaller-than-mainframe computers the ability to attach larger numbers of storage peripherals. This in turn allowed the smaller computers to maintain larger databases.

Technology moved rapidly and the peripherals themselves got smaller. These new smaller devices—tape and disk drives—could operate just as fast as their larger predecessors.

For example, the speed of the rotation of the disk in a disk drive increased. The speed of the access arms for the read/write heads also increased. And with both of these speeds increasing, that meant that the speed of data access increased.

The peripherals were just as fast and as reliable on the smaller computers as on the mainframes. And as these smaller computers became more popular, they were being used more and more for database applications and other immediate data access.

At this time, more and more people needed access to the data in real time. Real-time data is data that is accessed and updated or changed immediately, right now. For example, airline reservations and ticketing is a real-time application. There are only so many seats on an airplane; therefore you can sell only that many tickets. Reservation agents need to see immediately how many seats are available to determine how many tickets can be sold.

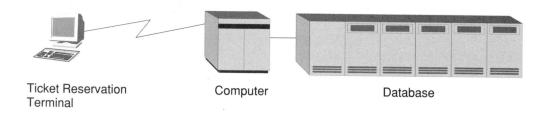

Ticket Reservation   Computer   Database
Terminal

Figure 2-5   Real-Time Access

In our example (Figure 2-5), the airline reservation ticket agent might need access to more than one airline's database. So the agent could be networked in to the different airlines' computers, allowing access to that airline's ticketing information held in the database for that particular airline. This is where networking began to evolve.

2.4 Local Area Networks (LANs)

Local Area (and Wide Area) Networks (LANs and WANs) began to grow rapidly because of the need to access data maintained on other computers.

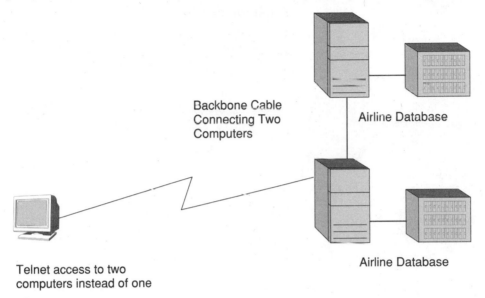

Backbone Cable
Connecting Two
Computers

Airline Database

Telnet access to two
computers instead of one

Airline Database

Figure 2-6   Early LANs

The ticket agent would have to acquire a logon identification from the owner of the other computer and permission to access their computer and database in order to accomplish this. Security of data became a big issue at this time, and still remains a big issue today.

LANs were created to enable the connection of one computer to another to allow users to access the data stored in the different databases on the connected computers (Figure 2-6). In the early days of networking, a computer was connected to the backbone cable. This was a thick cable that would be laid throughout a building so that all the computers in that building could be connected.

A more contemporary LAN still runs a cable through the building. Client workstations are connected to the LAN with hubs, and they can access the server and its stored data (Figure 2-7).

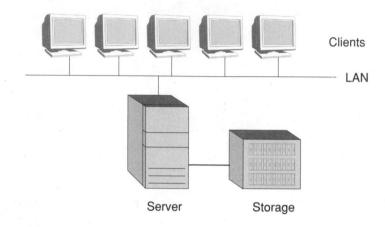

Figure 2-7   The Classic LAN

Of course, LANs were capable of considerable expansion.

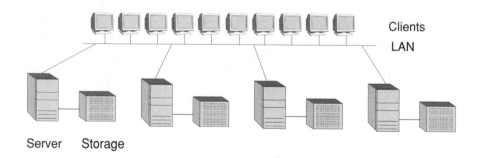

Figure 2-8   Multiple Computers on a LAN

In the example shown in Figure 2-8, the user can access data on any of the storage devices as long as he or she has a logon to the storage device's associated computer. For only one user, this arrangement would be very fast. However, if you bring too many users onto the LAN, demand becomes severe and the network begins to "bottleneck," or slow down.

What's the cause? The slowdown could be related to the speed of the processors, or the number of users requesting data at the same time, or the speed of the storage devices themselves.

The Network Administrator came onto the scene, proving that Information Technology creates at least as many jobs as it eliminates. With general responsibility for maintaining the health of the network, a specific Net Admin responsibility was identifying where the bottlenecks existed. To put it more delicately, performance optimization and capacity planning became key tasks for the Network Administrator.

2.5 Network Attached Storage

Another step in the development of storage solutions was (and is) Network Attached Storage (NAS). Network Attached Storage overcomes the limitations of attaching storage directly to the server. Devices are attached to the local area network to be used by systems on the LAN.

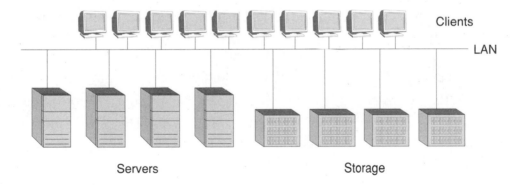

Figure 2-9   Network Attached Storage

NAS is available to any server on the network. By extension, data is available to any user, subject to security.

2.6 Mass Storage

It is a given that an enterprise stores more data today than ever before. There are large databases, and numerous, sizeable flat files. Operating systems and executables (programs) are also larger than ever before.

Mass storage consists of more and more disk drives, collected and connected together to provide the space necessary for the large files and databases.

It started by filling a server's drive bay with SCSI disk drives. This was (and is) called embedded storage. Of course, storage requirements outgrew this arrangement, so manufacturers had a great idea: directly attached storage.

With directly attached storage, you merely installed a SCSI host bus adapter in the server and strung multiple SCSI drives together along the bus. But the next step was to put six or eight disk drives together into a single structure, called an enclosure. And the enclosures grew bigger, until they could hold 10 disk drives, then 20, then 30, and on and on. The trend continued by connecting multiple enclosures on the bus.

The disks in these "disk farms" were highly independent of each other, and together they were "just a bunch of disks." This has given us one of the storage industry's best acronyms, JBOD ("Just a Bunch Of Disks"). SCSI JBODs remain a popular and effective method of attaching a lot of mass storage to a server.

Each of these disk drives could store massive amounts of data, "massive" being relative to the time. A big disk drive in the early 1990s might have been 500 MB in capacity. In the mid-1990s, we had passed the 1 GB, 2 GB, 4 GB, and 9 GB capacity points.

Currently, an HP JetStore 4000 disk enclosure holds six 9 GB or 18 GB drives, yielding up to 108 GB of storage. An SC60 disk enclosure has up to sixty 47 GB drives, providing about 2.8 TB.

2.6.1 Limitations of SCSI Mass Storage

Good as it sounds, the SCSI mass storage architecture has its limitations.

1. Limited speed. You might see 80 MBps on a good day.

2. Limited distance between devices. The SCSI cable limit is 25 meters.

3. Limited number of devices supported. The single-ended SCSI protocol
    is limited to 8 IDs or addresses per bus (7 devices and 1 controller), and
    wide differential SCSI is limited to 16 IDs per bus (15 devices and 1
    controller). Configuring a 1 TB disk storage unit, a fully redundant disk
    array would require 30 SCSI IDs (two per bus).

These concerns about limited speed, distance, and number of devices
caused the industry to start thinking about alternatives. The alternative is Fibre
Channel.

2.6.2 Fibre Channel

Fibre Channel is a relatively new communications protocol designed to
overcome the limitations of existing architectures. It is a generic data transport
mechanism with the primary task of transporting data at the fastest rate possible
using current technology. That rate is 1 Gbps or about 100 MBps. Fibre Channel
is a scalable interface for achieving high-speed data transfer rates among heterogeneous systems and peripherals. System types include supercomputers, mainframes, workstations, and desktops (PCs).

Peripherals include mass storage devices such as disk arrays and tape
libraries. Fibre Channel is a transport mechanism. It carries any number of existing protocols over a variety of physical media and existing cable options. But as
it turns out, SCSI over fiber optic cable is the most popular choice.

2.7 RAID

A chapter about the history of storage wouldn't be complete without a discussion of RAID technology. Yes, there can be vast collections of disk drives, but they are essentially defenseless against failure and data loss.

It argues, therefore, that, mass storage can't succeed without the benefits of a great protection scheme: RAID. Along with redundant components, a hardware RAID solution is a key performance feature for modern high-availability disk arrays.

RAID stands for Random Array of Independent Disks (also known as Random Array of Inexpensive Disks). RAID technology groups individual disk drives into a logical disk unit that functions as one or more virtual disks. This can improve reliability, performance, or both.

RAID uses parity data or disk mirroring to allow the disk array to continue operating without data loss after a disk failure. After the failed disk is replaced, the unit automatically rebuilds the lost data in the RAID group from information stored on the other disks in the group. The rebuilt RAID group contains a replica of information it would have held if the disk module had not failed. This is a key component of high availability.

There are different utilities that can be used to bind disk modules into logical disk units (called RAID groups).

The industry has defined the following RAID levels:

- RAID-0 (nonredundant individual access array)
- RAID-1 (mirrored pair)
- RAID-1/0 (mirrored RAID-0 group)
- RAID-3 (parallel access array)
- RAID-5 (individual access array)

2.7.1 RAID-0

RAID-0 is a performance solution, not a high availability solution. A RAID-0 group contains from 3 to 16 disk modules, and uses block striping. It spreads the data across the disk modules in the logical disk unit, and allows simultaneous I/Os to multiple disks.

Unlike the other RAID levels, RAID-0 doesn't provide any data redundancy, error recovery, or other high availability features. HP doesn't support RAID-0, because it doesn't provide redundancy.

2.7.2 RAID-1

A RAID-1 group consists of exactly two disk modules bound together as a mirrored pair. One disk is the data disk and the other is the disk mirror. The disk array hardware automatically writes the data to both the data disk and the disk mirror. Disk striping and parity are not used.

In a RAID-1 mirrored pair, if either the data disk or the disk mirror fails, the array uses the remaining disk for data recovery and continues operation until the failed disk can be replaced. If both disks fail, the RAID-1 mirrored pair becomes inaccessible.

RAID-1 is a high availability solution, but requires twice as many disks to store user data.

2.7.3 RAID-1/0

A RAID-1/0 group contains an even number of from 4 to 16 disk modules. Half of the disk modules are data disks and the other half are disk mirrors. Each disk mirror contains a copy of a data disk, so in essence, a RAID-1/0 group is a mirrored RAID-0 group.

A RAID-1/0 group uses block striping for performance and hardware mirroring for redundancy. The disadvantage of RAID level 1/0 is that the overhead cost is double that of RAID-0, because twice as many disk modules are required to store the user data, compared to a RAID-0 group.

When a data disk or a disk mirror fails, the disk array's processor automatically uses the remaining image for data recovery. A RAID-1/0 group can survive the failure of multiple disk modules, as long as one disk module (either the data disk or the disk mirror) in each pair of images continues to operate.

2.7.4   RAID-3

A RAID-3 group consists of 5 disk drives in a disk array, each on a separate internal single-ended SCSI-2 bus. RAID-3 uses disk striping over 4 disks for performance and a fifth, dedicated parity disk for redundancy.

When a failed disk drive is replaced, the disk array's storage processor automatically rebuilds the RAID group using the information stored on the remaining drives. If a data disk fails, the service processor automatically reconstructs all user data from the user data and parity information on the remaining disk modules. If the parity disk fails, the service processor reconstructs the parity information from the user data on the data disks.

Performance degrades while the service processor rebuilds the group, but the disk array continues to operate and all data is accessible during this time.

If 2 of the 5 disk modules in a RAID-3 group fail, the group becomes inaccessible. To guard against this, multiple global hot spares should be configured.

RAID-3 works well for applications using large block I/Os. It is not a good choice for transaction processing systems because the dedicated parity drive is a performance bottleneck. Whenever data is written to a data disk, a write must also be performed to the parity drive.

2.7.5   RAID-5

RAID-5 is usually the default configuration for HP disk arrays. It normally consists of 5 disk drives, but could contain from 3 to 16 drives. Like RAID-3, RAID-5 uses disk striping and parity, but it doesn't use a dedicated parity disk.

In a RAID-5 group, the hardware reads and writes parity information to each drive in the RAID group. For highest availability, the disk drives should each be on a separate internal single-ended SCSI-2 bus.

If a disk drive fails (or there's an internal SCSI bus failure), the disk array's storage processor reconstructs user data and parity information from the user data and parity information on the remaining drives.

Performance degrades while the service processor rebuilds the group, but the disk array continues to operate and all data is accessible during this time.

Like RAID-3, if 2 of the 5 disk modules in a RAID-5 group fail, the group becomes inaccessible. To guard against this, multiple global hot spares should be configured.

RAID-5 is good for multitasking environments. It has the same overhead cost as RAID-3 but provides faster random access because parity is spread across all drives in the RAID group. However, data transfers are a little slower than RAID-3, but that can be helped if the disk array has caching capabilities.

2.7.6 Disk Striping

Disk striping is a technique where data is written to and read from uniformly sized segments across all disk drives in a RAID group simultaneously and independently. The uniformly sized segments are called block stripes.

Hardware disk striping can be implemented by configuring the disk drives in a RAID-1/0 group, a RAID-3 group, or a RAID-5 group. By allowing multiple sets of read/write heads to work on the same I/O operation at the same time, disk striping can enhance performance.

The amount of information simultaneously written to or read from each drive is the stripe element size. The default stripe element size is 128 sectors of 512 bytes per sector or 65,536 bytes (except for RAID-3 groups, whose stripe element size is fixed at one sector and can't be modified). The stripe element size is configurable and can affect the performance of RAID groups.

The smaller the stripe element size, the more efficient is the distribution of data written or read across the stripes on the disks in the RAID group. The best stripe element size is the smallest size that will only rarely force I/Os to a second stripe. The stripe size should be an even multiple of 16 sectors (8 KB). The stripe element size becomes an integral part of the logical disk unit and can't be changed without unbinding the RAID group and losing all data on it.

The stripe size is the number of data disks in a RAID group multiplied by the stripe element size. For example, if the stripe element size is the default size of 128 sectors and the RAID group comprises 5 disk modules, the stripe size is 128 x 5, or 640 sectors (327,680 bytes).

2.7.7 Mirroring

Mirroring maintains a duplicate copy of a logical disk image on another disk drive. The copy is called a disk mirror. If either the original data disk or the disk mirror is inaccessible, the other disk provides continuous access to the data. The disk array continues running on the good image without interruption. There are two kinds of mirroring:

- Hardware mirroring, in which the disk array controller automatically and transparently synchronizes the two disk images without user or operating system involvement

- Software mirroring, in which the host operating system software synchronizes the disk images

You can create a hardware mirror by binding disk drives as a RAID-1 mirrored pair or a RAID-1/0 group. The disk array controller mirrors the data automatically and, in the event of a disk failure, rebuilds the data from the remaining disk image.

Using software mirroring, RAID-0 groups or individual disk units with no inherent data redundancy can be mirrored. The operating system mirrors the images.

2.7.8 Parity

Parity is a data protection feature that makes data highly available. Parity data makes it possible for a RAID group to survive a number of failures without losing user data.

- If one data disk module fails, the disk array controller can reconstruct the user data from the remaining user data and parity information.

- If the parity disk fails, the parity information can be recalculated from the data disks.

- If each disk in a RAID group is bound on a separate internal bus and one bus fails, the disk on it is inaccessible. After the bus fault is cleared, the disk array controller can rebuild the RAID group from the user and parity information stored on the disks on the other buses.

In all three cases, the rebuilt RAID group contains a replica of the information it would have contained had the disk module or bus not failed.

Parity is calculated on each write I/O by doing a serial binary exclusive OR of the data segments in the stripe written to the data disks in the RAID group. For example, in a RAID group of five disk modules, the data segment written on the first disk is exclusive OR'ed (XOR'ed) with the data segment written on the second disk. The result is exclusive OR'ed with the write segment on the third disk, which is exclusive OR'ed with the write segment on the fourth disk. The result, which is the parity of the write segment, is written to the fifth disk of the RAID group.

RAID-3 and RAID-5 groups maintain parity data that lets a disk group survive one disk failure without losing data. The group can also survive a single internal bus failure if each disk in the RAID group is bound on a separate internal bus.

2.7.9 Global Hot Spares

The availability of all RAID groups in the disk array can be increased by using one or more disks as global hot spares. A global hot spare is a dedicated, online, backup disk used by the disk array as an automatic replacement disk when a disk in a RAID group fails. Hot spares cannot be used to store user data during normal disk array operations; after all, they are spares. When any disk in a RAID group fails, the disk array controller automatically begins rebuilding the failed disk's structure on a global hot spare. And when the disk array controller finishes this rebuild process, the disk group functions as usual, using the global hot spare as a replacement for the failed disk.

After the failed disk has been replaced with a new disk, the disk array controller starts copying the data from the former global hot spare onto the new disk. When the copy onto the replacement disk is completed, the disk array controller automatically frees the global hot spare to serve as a global hot spare again.

A global hot spare is most useful when the highest data availability is a requirement. It reduces the risk of a second disk failure. It also eliminates the time and effort needed for an operator to notice that a disk has failed, find a suitable replacement, remove the failed disk, and install the replacement. Multiple global hot spares can be configured in environments where data availability is crucial. This helps ensure that data remains accessible if multiple disks fail in a RAID group.

2.8 Storage Area Networks (SANs)

The evolution of storage brings us to Storage Area Networks (SANs), described in detail in Chapter 4.

A Storage Area Network is based on the principle of networking devices together. As you learned in Chapter 1, the SAN consists of a group of mass storage devices (disk arrays and tape libraries) connected indirectly to host computer systems and each other by means of interconnecting devices such as hubs or switches.

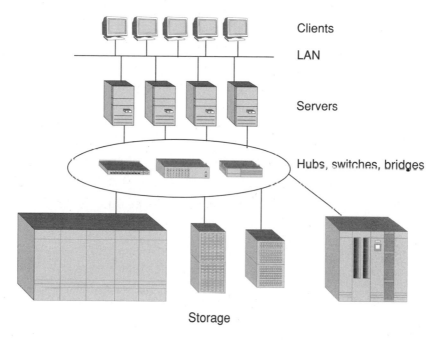

Figure 2-10   Example of a SAN

Where LANs connect host computer systems together to share the access to servers and stored data, SANs connect storage devices together to provide host computer systems (and users) high-speed and immediate access to data. SANs also provide host computer systems multiple routes to data, as a measure of protection if failures happen. In some LANs where SANs are employed, the host computer system in control of some specific data can be "failed over" to another host system to guarantee access to data in case of a system failure. It can be configured so that any host can access any storage unit.

CHAPTER 3

A Brief Review of Fibre Channel

This chapter discusses:

- **Limitations of current mass storage architectures**
- **How Fibre Channel answers these limitations**
- **Advantages of Fibre Channel**
- **Fibre Channel basics**
- **Topologies**
- **Fibre Channel functional levels and protocols**
- **Fibre Channel Arbitrated Loop (FC-AL)**
- **Hubs and topologies**

Fibre Channel is the enabling technology of the SAN. This chapter explains the significant concepts.

3.1   Current Mass Storage Architectures

Current data transfer protocols (such as IPI, HIPPI, and SCSI) have problems that limit their effectiveness in mass storage. The limitations, illustrated in Figure 3-1, are:

1. Limited speed
2. Limited distance between devices
3. Limited number of devices supported

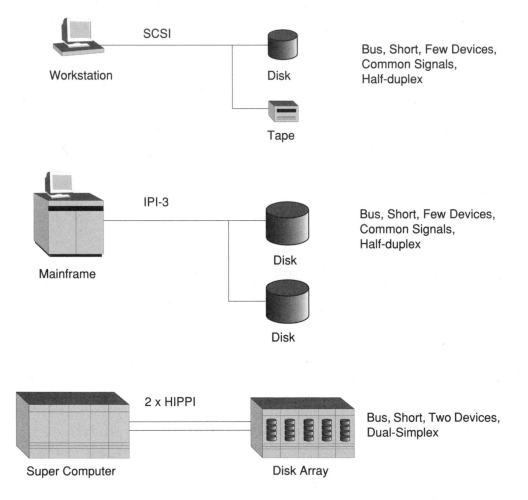

Figure 3-1   Current Limitations

For example, the Small Computer System Interface (SCSI) is restricted to:

- the bus being no longer than 25 meters
- 32 SCSI devices per bus
- a double cable system

In today's modern computer system environments, these restrictions are both very limiting to design and confining in space—and it gets worse. The two-byte wide SCSI P-cable limits configurations to 16 devices.

The single-ended SCSI protocol is limited to eight IDs or addresses per bus (seven devices and one controller), and wide differential SCSI is limited to 16 IDs per bus (15 devices and one controller) to configure a one-terabyte disk storage unit. A fully redundant disk array would require 30 SCSI IDs (two per bus).

These concerns about limited speed, distance, and number of devices caused the industry to start thinking about alternatives. The alternative is Fibre Channel.

3.2   How Does Fibre Channel Help?

Fibre Channel is a new communications protocol designed to overcome the limitations of existing architectures. It is a generic data transport mechanism with the primary task of transporting data at the fastest rate possible using current technology. Fibre Channel is a scalable interface for achieving high-speed data transfer rates among heterogeneous systems and peripherals. System types include supercomputers, mainframes, workstations, and desktop PCs.

Peripherals include mass storage devices such as disk arrays and possibly tape libraries. The main purpose of Fibre Channel is to have any number of existing protocols over a variety of physical media and existing cable options.

Table 3-1 shows the various speeds and distances that can be attained using different cable types.

Table 3-1   Cable Types, Speeds, and Distances

SPEED (Mbps)	9 µm Single Mode	50 µm Multimode	62.5 µm Multimode	COAX	Mini COAX	TWINAX	STP
133				100 m	42 m	93 m	80 m
266	10 km	2 km	1 km	100 m	28 m	66 m	57 m
533	10 km	1 km	1km	71 m	19 m	46 m	48 m
1063	10 km	500 m	175 m	50 m	14 m	33 m	28 m
2125	2 km	500 m					
4250	2 km	175 m					

3.2.1   Fibre Channel Use for Mass Storage

Since Fibre Channel is a generic data transport mechanism, it can transmit a number of existing networking and I/O protocols:

I/O protocols:

- SCSI
- HIPPI
- IPI

Network protocols:

- IP
- IEEE 802.2

Hewlett-Packard has chosen to support the SCSI-3 protocol over Fibre Channel for its mass storage environment. Mass storage consists of several device classes:

- tapes

- disks

- disk arrays

3.3   Advantages of Fibre Channel for Mass Storage

There are some definite advantages to using Fibre Channel over other architectures. Although this is not an all-inclusive list, these are the major advantages:

3.3.1   Distance

Hewlett-Packard supports up to 10,000 meters (10 km) between the computer (or system) and the peripheral. What this means is that between the computer and the peripheral there can be a distance of 10 kilometers. Section 3.5 will describe this in more detail, however, the distance advantage is an excellent solution for the campus-type environment.

3.3.2   Speed

Fibre Channel permits a theoretical speed of up to 4000 Mbps. (As mentioned previously, Hewlett-Packard supports 1063 Mbps.) Speeds depend greatly on the design of the pieces and parts that are connected within the topology between the computer and the peripheral. Our challenge within the industry now is to determine how to achieve these higher speeds allowed by the Fibre Channel standard. This speaks directly to performance, because with the speeds capable with Fibre Channel throughput increases by four or five times over current channels.

3.3.3   Connectivity and Scalability

Computer system environments today are very limited in the number of devices that can be connected together. They are also limited in that today's configurations do not easily allow the introduction of new technologies, protocols, or even different protocols simultaneously.

Fibre Channel addresses these issues by allowing:

- from 2 to over 16 million ports that can be concurrently logged in to a fabric with the 24-bit address identifier

- the introduction of new technologies like laser light

- the transportation of different protocols simultaneously

3.4 Fibre Channel Basics

Fibre Channel has a number of new terms having no previous association with other protocols. For example, SCSI has Initiators and Targets, and Fibre Channel has Originators and Responders. In Fibre Channel, the Originators are devices that originate (initiate) a transaction or operation. The Responders then, answer the operation of the Originators. Also refer to the glossary in the back of this book for complete definitions of all terms.

The following pages will describe more terms, as well as the names of some of the pieces and parts of Fibre Channel technology/topologies. A node is a device. A device is any processor or mass storage subsystem with Fibre Channel functionality. A node has at least one port (in N_Port, the "N" stands for node) and can have multiple ports. A port is the connecting interface between the cable and the device, located on the device. The cable is referred to as the link. Fibre Channel is based on full duplex operation. Therefore two fibers, (TX and RX) one to transmit and one to receive, are required to operate a port. The term fiber in this case can be a copper cable or an optical strand cable.

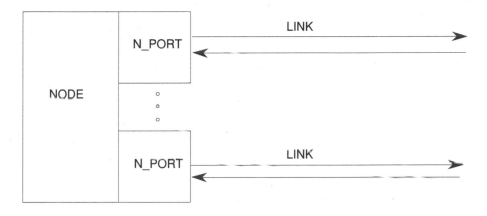

Figure 3-2 Basic Terms: Node, Port, and Link

3.5 Topologies

3.5.1 Point-to-Point

The first topology to discuss is the simplest. It is called a point-to-point topology. It is two nodes (devices) connected together. One node could be a computer system and the other node could be a disk array.

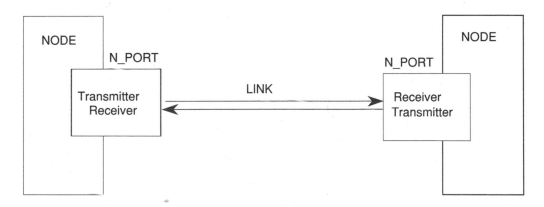

Figure 3-3 Point-to-Point Topology

This topology uses two nodes (each node must have at least one port), and the nodes are connected using one link or cable. The point-to-point connection guarantees instant access with no interference from any other node or application.

If a peripheral node, such as a disk array, has two N_Ports, access to the disk array could be shared between two computer systems. For example, the disk array could act as a repository of common software for two computer systems. This would be considered two point-to-point connections. See Figure 3-4.

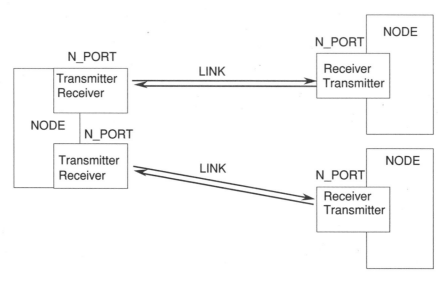

Figure 3-4   Two Point-to-Point Connections

A point-to-point connection may also be considered a two-node loop. Hewlett-Packard's implementation of point-to-point is a two-node loop. This brings us to our next topology.

3.5.2   Arbitrated Loop

A loop, called Fibre Channel Arbitrated Loop (FC-AL), can have up to 127 ports connected in series (one right after the other) continuing around and back to the originator. For example, the node 1 transmitter is connected to the node 2 receiver, the node 2 transmitter is connected to the node 3 receiver, and so on, until the final node transmitter is connected to the node 1 receiver, thus completing the loop. Figure 3-5 illustrates this example.

A node loop port (NL_Port) wins arbitration on the loop and establishes a connection with another NL_Port on the loop. At the time the connection is established it is considered to be a point-to-point connection or two-node loop.

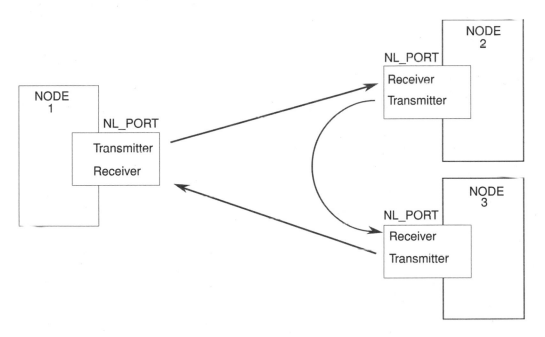

Figure 3-5 Arbitrated Loop Topology

In an arbitrated loop only the two connected ports can communicate at any given time. All the other ports act as repeaters. When the communication comes to an end between the two connected ports, the loop becomes available for arbitration and a new connection may be established. Fairness is provided for during arbitration to provide equal access to all ports. The FC-AL features, operations, and implementations will be discussed in further detail later in this chapter.

3.5.3   Switch Topology or Fabric

The switch topology uses the concept of fabric. The fabric is a mesh of connections. When attached to a fabric, a single N_Port can access all the rest, including members of loops.

Unlike the FC-AL topology, many connections may be established within the fabric. It can be compared to a telephone system where many phone calls may be occurring all at the same time.

Any node can be attached to a fabric through the N or NL_Ports by way of a link. The port in the fabric is called an F_Port. An N_Port attaches to an F_Port. If an NL_Port is attached to a fabric, then the fabric port is an FL_Port.

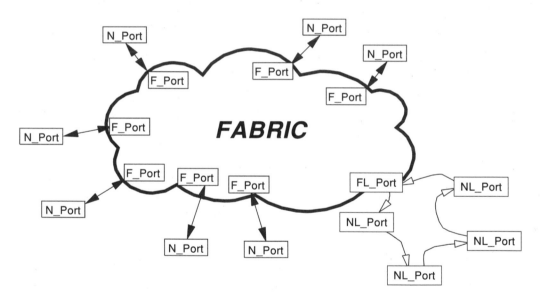

Figure 3-6   Fabric Topology

3.6 Fibre Channel Functional Levels and Protocols

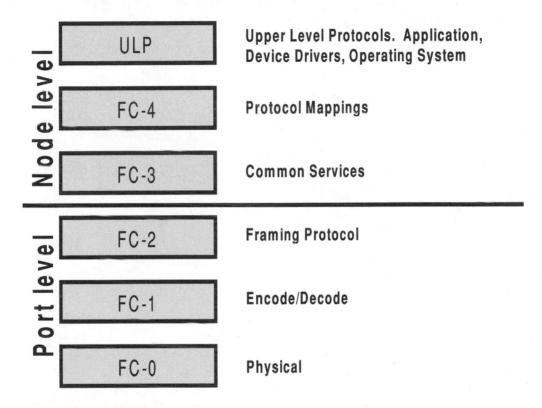

Figure 3-7   Fibre Channel Protocol Functional Levels

3.7 Functional Levels

Fibre Channel Protocol (FCP) functional levels are FC-0 through FC-4. The FC-3 and FC-4 levels are outside the port level, permitting the sharing of resources of several ports in the event of future extensions. Applications lie above the FC-4 level. For example, the peripheral drivers for a SCSI application that typically communicates with Host Bus Adapters (HBAs) will communicate with the FC-4 level.

3.7.1   Placement in a Topology

As shown in Figure 3-8, FC-0, FC-1, and FC-2 are implemented at the port level. FC-3, FC-4, and the Upper Level Protocols (ULPs) are implemented at the node level. Fibre Channel considers that which is not visible on the link (above the FC-0 physical level) to be system dependent, and simply identifies the functions to be performed. It does not require allocation or placement.

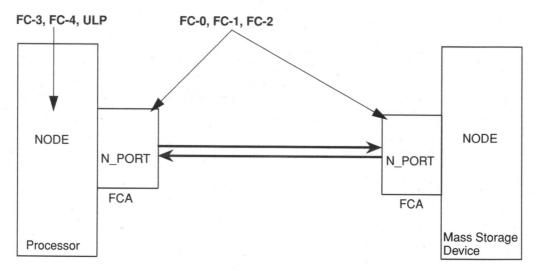

Figure 3-8   Placement in a Topology

Figure 3-8 shows an example of a simple point-to-point (two-node loop) topology to identify where the functionality of each level resides. FC-0, FC-1, and FC-2 are all implemented at the Port level. This means that each Port has the functionality of these levels. FC-3, FC-4, and ULPs are all implemented at the Node level.

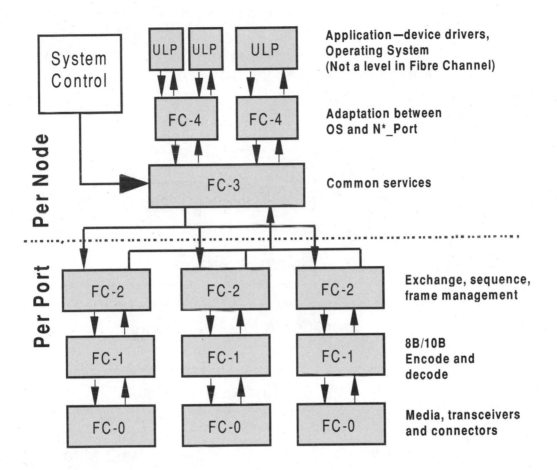

Figure 3-9   Functional Levels

Figure 3-9 shows another way to demonstrate this. The horizontal line in the middle divides the Node from the Port. You will see something new in this figure. Where there are multiples of FC-0, FC-1, and FC-2, there is only one FC-3, the common services level. That is because the FC-3 functionality may interact with multiple ports on a node. And then again above the FC-3 level, there are multiple FC-4s and ULPs. That is because there may be multiple ULPs within a node that map through multiple FC-4s.

Figure 3-10 shows yet more detail. This figure shows that there are five levels used by Fibre Channel, (FC-0 through FC-4) separating the Upper Level Protocols into the system interface. Also, you can see that FC-4 can accommodate not only the channel protocols of SCSI, IPI, and others, but can also accommodate network protocols like IEEE 802.2.

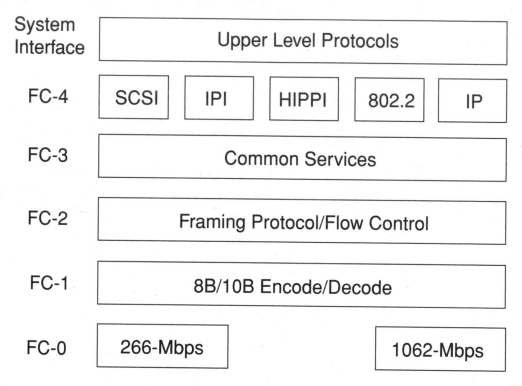

Figure 3-10   Fibre Channel Framing Levels

Now you have a good overview of the different functional levels within Fibre Channel. Continue on to the next section to read about the detailed characteristics of each level.

3.8 FC-0: The Physical Layer

Level FC-0 deals with the physical variants:

- fiber
- connectors
- receivers
- data encoders/decoders
- serializers/deserializers
- transmitters

FC-0 deals strictly with the serial bit stream to be sent and received, and the conductors used to transmit that stream. This layer is called the physical layer. The Fibre Channel standard calls this function the Link Control Facility (LCF). The requirements are different for different types of media and different data rates.

3.8.1   Connectors

Remember, Chapter 1 stated that the main purpose of Fibre Channel is to have any number of existing protocols over a variety of physical media and existing cable options. Therefore, FC-0 provides for four types of connectors to accommodate for the variety of physical media, and for possible existing cable.

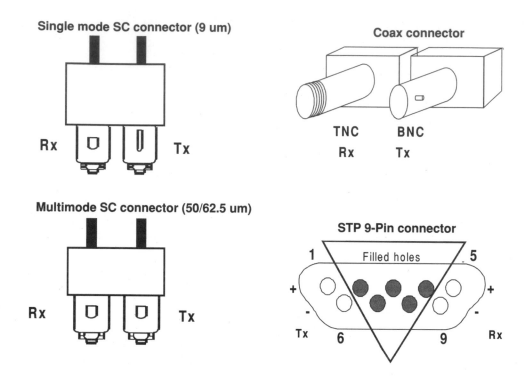

Figure 3-11   Connectors

The single mode and multimode connectors connect to fiber optic cable. Single mode fiber optic cable is thinner and has less bandwidth than multimode cable. Therefore, single mode cable is used for long-distance transmissions—10,000 meters (10 km)—while multimode cable is used for shorter distances, 500 meters.

An example for use might be to connect two buildings some distance away from each other with single mode fiber optic cable. Then, within each building, connect each floor using multimode cable.

A word of caution, when working in a mixed environment of single and multimode cabling: be aware that the connectors have been keyed to prevent accidental connection of single mode to multimode or the reverse. However, the keying of the connectors is not perfect nor completely standardized. Also, multimode fiber cable does not work with single mode transmitters and receivers. The single mode light "rattles around" in the big 50 or 62.5 um fibers and dissipates quickly, causing data loss.

The Fibre Channel standard does provide for connections to coax and copper cabling.

For coax cable:

- the TNC for receive

- the BNC for transmit

For copper cable the shielded twisted-pair (STP), 9-pin D-type connector (DB9), is used. To prevent accidental attachments, the middle five holes in the Fibre Channel DB9 female connector are filled.

3.8.1.1   OFC and Non-OFC

Open Fibre Control (OFC) is a safety feature used to prohibit the laser light from functioning when there is a break or disconnect in the fiber cable. This is used specifically with high-intensity laser lights. Hewlett-Packard uses non-OFC because the lasers are of low intensity. Therefore, the laser light is not turned off when there is a disconnect.

However, this does not mean you should look at or point the fiber cable directly at your eye, since there still could be some damage. When checking a fiber cable to see if a laser light exists, point the cable end at a white piece of paper. If a red dot appears on the paper, the transmitting laser is functioning.

3.8.1.2   Wavelength

Wavelength is a topic related to single and multimode connectors. Longwave lasers are used for long Fibre Channel links, from approximately 500 to 10,000 meters. They are typically used with single mode fiber of a 9-micron core size.

Shortwave lasers are used for FC-AL links, up to approximately 500 meters. They are typically used with multimode fiber. The preferred fiber core size is 50-micron. 62.5-micron core size is also supported for compatibility with existing FDDI installations. However, fiber of this type has smaller bandwidth and, in this case, the distance is limited by the fiber bandwidth. The length recommendation for the 62.5-micron fiber cable is 175 meters.

When pulling new cable, it is recommended that the customer pull both 9- and 50-micron cable to accommodate future expansion.

3.9   FC-1: The Transmission Protocol Level

The FC-1 level defines the transmission protocol including the 8B/10B encode/decode scheme, byte synchronization, and character-level error control. This protocol uses the 8B/10B encoding scheme that encodes 8-bit bytes into 10-bit transmission characters. The 8B/10B encoding was developed by IBM, and determined to be the best for the expected error rate of the system.

The 8B/10B code has outstanding line characteristics, including long transmission distances and very good error-detection capability. The 8B/10B code finds errors that a parity check cannot detect. Parity does not find even numbers of bit errors, only odd numbers. But 8B/10B finds almost all errors. Fibre Channel also employs a Cyclic Redundancy Check (CRC) on transmitted data. This also assists with error detection.

To assist with transmission the 8B/10B code uses 12 special characters. However, we are only concerned with one, the 28.5 special character. At present, it is the only special character used by Fibre Channel in the 8B/10B code.

3.9.1   8B/10B Encoding

The format of the 8B/10B character is *Ann.m*, where:

- *A* is equal to "D" for data or "K" for a special character

- *nn* is the decimal value of the lower five bits of a byte (bits EDCBA)

- "." is the ASCII period character

- *m* is the decimal value of the upper three bits of a byte (bits HGF)

Figure 3-12 shows the translation of the HEX number 45.

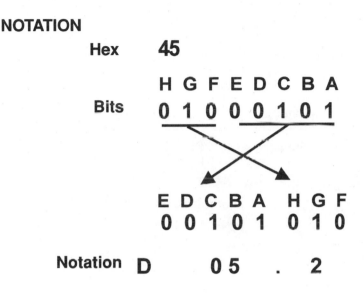

Figure 3-12 8B/10B Encoding

The 8B/10B encoded bytes have a property known as disparity, which can be positive, negative, or neutral. An 8B/10B byte has negative disparity if there are more binary ones in the byte than binary zeroes. Conversely, the byte has positive disparity if there are more binary zeroes than ones. Neutral disparity is when the number of binary ones equals the number of binary zeroes.

3.9.2   K28.5 Special Character Encoding

The *K28.5* special character has the following components:

- K stands for special character
- 28 is the decimal value of bits EDCBA—11100
- "." is the ASCII period character
- 5 is the decimal value of bits HGF—101

Figure 3-13 shows the translation of the HEX number BC.

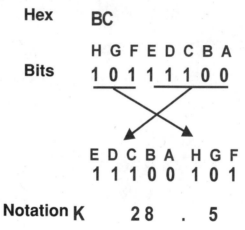

NOTATION

Hex	BC

```
          H G F E D C B A
Bits      1 0 1 1 1 1 0 0
```

```
          E D C B A   H G F
          1 1 1 0 0   1 0 1
```

Notation K   2 8 . 5

TRANSMISSION ORDER

```
8B/10B  A B C D E   F G H
        a b c d e i f g h j
        0 0 1 1 1 1 1 0 1 0   (RD-)
    OR  1 1 0 0 0 0 0 1 0 1   (RD+)
```

Figure 3-13   8B/10B Translation

3.9.3   FC-1 Transmission Word

A transmission word is composed of four transmission characters. Remember, the 8B/10B code encoded an 8-bit byte into a 10-bit character. Therefore, a transmission word is a 40-bit group of four 10B transmission characters. A transmission word can be one of two kinds:

- Data—The first transmission character is an encoded data byte

- Ordered Set—The fourth transmission character is the K28.5 special character

If the transmission word is data, each of the four transmission characters is an encoded data byte. If the transmission word is an ordered set, the first byte is a K28.5 transmission character. The other three transmission characters are normal encoded data bytes. Ordered sets permit control functions to be imbedded in the bit stream. One simple use of ordered sets is to determine at a receiver where word boundaries are. If all transmission words are data transmission words, the receiver has only a 2.5% chance of getting it right (that is, 1 in 40 bits).

3.9.4   FC-1: Ordered Set

An ordered set is a transmission word beginning with a special character— as previously discussed, the K28.5 character. Because this special character is present, this transmission word has a special control function meaning. There are three possible meanings:

- Frame delimiter—This defines what class of service is required. (Classes of service will be explained later in this chapter.) The frame contains a start of frame (SOF) and an end of frame (EOF) delimiter.

- Primitive signals—There are two kinds of primitive signals:

  - The ordered set may be a primitive signal used for buffer-to-buffer flow control.

  - There is an ordered set for idle primitives. Idles are words that fill the space between frames. In Fibre Channel, the transmitter must continuously send something over the media. This helps preserve bit, byte, and word synchronization, and permits faster communication.

- Primitive sequences—A set of three identical ordered sets used for link control. These are intended for notification of link failures and loss of synchronization.

3.10 FC-2: Framing Protocol

The FC-2 framing protocol manages flow control so data will be delivered with no collisions or loss. This level defines the signaling protocol, including the frame and byte structure, which is the data transport mechanism used by Fibre Channel. The framing protocol is used to break sequences into individual frames for transmission, flow control, 32-bit CRC generation, and various classes of service.

To aid in data transfer, FC-2 provides for the following elements:

- Frames—basic units of information transfer. The maximum payload of a frame is 2112 bytes.

- Sequences—are made up of one or more frames. FC-2 names each sequence and tracks it to completion.

- Exchanges—are the largest construct understood by FC-2. An exchange is a unidirectional or bidirectional set of nonconcurrent sequences. SCSI-3 FCP uses bidirectional exchanges, with information passing in one direction at a time. To send data in the opposite direction, sequence initiative is passed from one port to another and back again. Each port generates one or more sequences within the exchange.

- Packets—are made up of one or more exchanges.

3.10.1   Frame Structure

Figure 3-14 demonstrates frame structure.

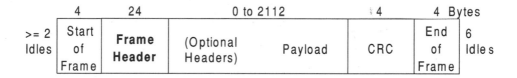

Figure 3-14   FC-2 Frame Structure

The total length of the frame is 2148 transmission characters or 537 transmission words. The SOF, CRC, and EOF are all one transmission word in length with the frame header being six transmission words in length. The frame is followed by a minimum of 6 idles (or 24 transmission characters).

3.10.2   Frame Header Structure

The frame header is divided into fields to carry control information. Figure 3-15 shows these fields.

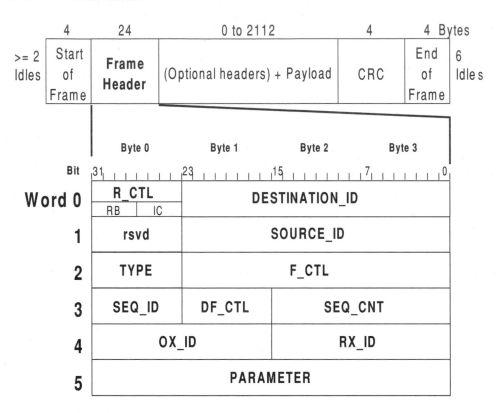

Figure 3-15   Frame Header Structure

Table 3-2 describes each of the fields in the frame header.

Table 3-2   Frame Header Structure Explanations

Routing Control (R_CTL)	Contains IC (Information Category) and RB (Routing Bits) subfields. Routing Bits indicate the frame type. The IC field indicates payload content (for example, SCSI status).
Destination ID (D_ID)	The native address of the destination N_Port, a well-known address, or an alias address.
Source ID (S_ID)	The address identifier of the source N_Port.
Type	The protocol associated with the payload (for example, SCSI-3).
Frame Control (F_CTL)	Bits that identify the transfer of sequence; beginning, middle, or end of sequence; and end of connection.
Data Field Control (DF_CTL)	Indicates the presence of optional headers.
Sequence ID (SEQ_ID)	A unique numeric sequence identifier between two ports.
Sequence Count (SEQ_CNT)	A 16-bit rollover frame counter or frame identifier.
Originator Exchange ID (OX_ID)	A number an exchange originator uses to uniquely identify an exchange.
Responder Exchange ID (RX_ID)	A number like OX_ID, but for the exchange responder.
Parameter	Contents may vary with frame type. Often used as a relative offset of payload contents.

3.11 FC-3: Common Services

The FC-3 level, located at the center of the functional levels, concerns itself with functions spanning multiple N_Ports. The FC-3 level is the single point in the architecture through which all traffic must flow in both directions. The FC-3 level will contain services common (available) to all ports on a node.

A node may have several ports. A node may also have several ULPs and FC-4 level mappings. However, there is only one FC-3 Common Services level per node. The FC-3 level can manage a set of tables holding the login information for other active ports. Each port on the FC-3 level knows which ports are busy and which exchanges they are busy with.

Figure 3-9 on page 57 shows where the FC-3 level fits into the overall scheme of all the Fibre Channel levels.

Currently there are three functions defined within the FC-3 level standard:

- Striping—Used to achieve higher bandwidth. Striping allows multiple links simultaneously and transmits a single information unit across multiple links employing multiple N_Ports in parallel.

- Hunt Groups—Are a group of N_Ports associated with a single node. They permit any N_Port on the node to receive information containing the correct alias identifier.

- Multicast—This can be compared to a broadcast message. It allows a single information unit to be transmitted to multiple N_Ports on a node.

The FC-3 level knows nothing about the topology of Fibre Channel or the physical signaling at the lower levels. This is handled by FC-1 and FC-2 levels. FC-3 understands if there are multiple ports attached to a node and if they may participate in multiport operations like multicasting.

Knowing which ports are busy allows the FC-3 level to route exchanges between two N*_Ports and FC-4s.

3.12 FC-4: Mapping

Mapping is a set of rules that is defined to move information from the Upper Level Protocol interfaces to the lower Fibre Channel levels. The ANSI SCSI committee and the Fibre Channel committees are working on defining these rules.

Currently, the rules provide for transforming information units into Fibre Channel sequences and exchanges and back again. When fully developed, these mapping rules are intended to provide clear mapping instructions between the Upper Level Protocol (ULP) and the FC-3 and FC-2 levels to enhance interoperability between applications.

To send data, the FC-4 level takes a unit of information (this is the payload in a frame and is the actual data that is being transmitted, it is referred to as an Information Unit (IU)) from a ULP and transforms it into sequences for the FC-3 and FC-2 levels. To receive data, the FC-4 level takes a sequence from the FC-3 and FC-2 levels and transforms it into an IU for the ULP.

3.13 Upper Level Protocols

The ULPs allow two devices to communicate. For example, a computer sends data to a disk to be stored for later use, or the communication that takes place in a client/server relationship.

There are many standards currently defined that have been in use for years that enable interoperation, such as SCSI or IPI. A goal of Fibre Channel is to provide a structure where legacy ULPs would continue to operate, preserving the software developed in the past. In this regard then, a map will exist in the FC-4 level for every ULP that is transportable over Fibre Channel.

3.14 Classes of Service

Fibre Channel classes of service are managed by the FC-2 level. Currently the following five classes of service are defined by the standard:

- Class 1—Dedicated connection service.
  - Connection-oriented
  - Acknowledged delivery

- Class 2—Multiplexed service.
  - Connectionless
  - Acknowledged delivery

- Class 3—Datagram service. The device drivers determine if data is not received and needs to be retransmitted.
  - Connectionless
  - Unacknowledged delivery

- Class 4—Fractional service. It uses a fraction of the bandwidth of the link between two ports for communication.
  - Connection-oriented

- Class 6—Unidirectional Dedicated Connection service. It provides dedicated unidirectional connections.
  - Connection-oriented

Classes 4 and 6 are defined, but are not widely implemented. Other classes of service may follow. However, they are currently not defined.

3.15 FC-AL Characteristics

There are three topologies supported by Fibre Channel: loop, point-to-point, and switched. FC-AL is the loop topology that will be discussed here. The Fibre Channel Arbitrated Loop (FC-AL) is a means by which to connect up to 126 devices in a serial loop configuration.

In the FC-AL, each port discovers when it has been attached to a loop. Addresses are assigned automatically on initialization. Access to the loop is arbitrated; there are no collisions and there is no single permanent loop master.

FC-AL permits fair access on a single arbitrated loop. Access fairness means every port wanting to initiate traffic will have the opportunity to own the loop and initiate traffic before any other port has the opportunity to own the loop for the second time.

3.15.1   Types of Loops

3.15.1.1   FC-AL Private Loop

A private loop is enclosed and known only to itself. Figure 3-16 demonstrates a common configuration used with FC-AL for Fibre Channel Mass Storage. In this example, the processor node only has one Fibre Channel host bus adapter (HBA).

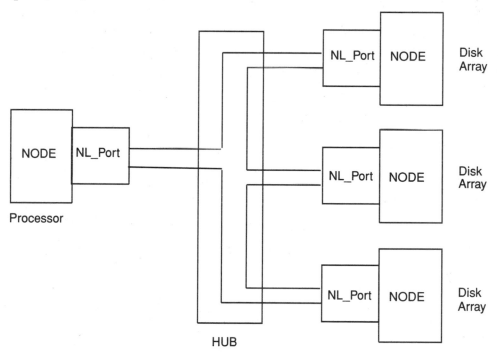

Figure 3-16   FC-AL Private Loop

The processor node is connected to the hub. Then the three devices—in this case disk arrays—are connected to the hub and the loop is formed. If the hub is not used, the connection with all three disk arrays cannot be made. A connection to only one, in point-to-point fashion, could be accomplished. Another option would be to install three HBAs into the processor node and connect each to a disk array separately.

The hub, then, provides an advantage in saving HBA slots in the processor node and allows multiple storage devices to be added to the loop.

3.15.1.2   FC-AL Public Loop

A public loop, shown in Figure 3-17, requires a fabric and has at least one FL_Port connecting to a fabric. A public loop extends the reach of the loop topology by attaching the loop to a fabric. Public loops are a way to leverage the cost of one switched connection over many devices in a loop. Connecting a loop to a fabric is similar to connecting a local area network (LAN) to a wide area network (WAN). The fabric is usually represented by a cloud, as shown in Figure 3-18.

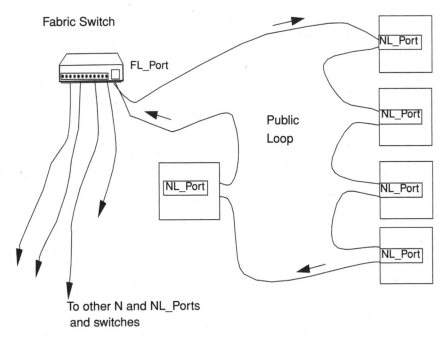

Figure 3-17   FC-AL Public Loop

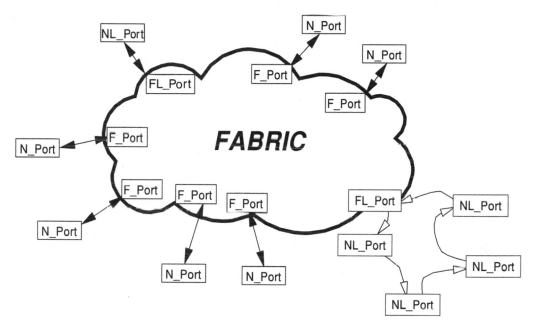

Figure 3-18   FC-AL Fabric

3.16 Operation of the FC-AL

3.16.1   Primitive Signals

Primitive signals are sent by a transmitting port, and recognized and acted on by a receiving port.

Table 3-3   Primitive Signals

Signal	Description
ARB(x)	Arbitrate address x for loop control
OPN(y)	Open one other NL_Port - Full duplex - Half duplex
OPN(r)	Replicate - Broadcast - Selective replicate or multicast
CLS	Close the circuit at the NL_Port
MRK(tx)	Synchronization signal "t" from "x"

Note:
The 'x' is the address of the port wanting to own the loop and the "y" is the address of the port to be opened.

3.16.2   Primitive Sequences

Primitive sequences are not recognized or acted on until the third consecutive occurrence of the ordered set. Currently, there are only three primitive sequences used:

- LIP   Loop Initialization

- LPB   Loop Port Bypass

- LPE   Loop Port Enable

The LIP sequence allows for discovery of ports on the loop. This means that when a new node is connected to a loop, the LIP sequence discovers it and allows for the new node to be initialized on the loop.

3.16.3   Arbitrated Loop Physical Address (AL_PA)

All ports have a 24-bit native address identifier, called the N_Port ID. The AL_PA is in the lower eight (8) bits of this identifier. The lower the 8-bit address, the higher the priority is for arbitrating. An 8-bit field can have values from 0–255, or 256 values. However, not all of these are used for physical addresses.

AL_PA values must have neutral disparity. (Remember that 8B/10B encoding has positive, negative, or neutral disparity.) There are only 134 neutral disparity values out of the set of 256 8-bit addresses. 126 values, of the 134, are used for port addresses and 8 are used for control functions. Hewlett-Packard uses addresses 00-EF. See Table 3-4 for further reference.

The upper 16 bits are non-zero for public ports on a public loop but are zero for ports on a private loop. This is how the loop determines whether it is talking publicly or privately.

Table 3-4   AL_PA Values

Value	Description
00	Reserved for FL_Port (high priority)
01-EF	Available for active NL_Ports (126 valid neutral disparity values)
F0	Reserved for access fairness algorithm (lowest priority)
F1-F6	Invalid
F7	Used with initialization primitive sequences
F8	Used with initialization primitive sequences
F9-FE	Reserved (3 valid)
FF	Replicate request (low priority) or to address "ALL"

3.16.4   Loop States and Operation

3.16.4.1 Operation Overview

There is a controlled arbitration process for a port to gain control of an arbitrated loop. The Open NL_Port selects a destination NL_Port on the loop before a frame is transmitted. The arbitrating port releases control of the loop when frame transmission is complete.

A port gains ownership of the loop by an arbitration process. The port winning arbitration sends an OPN primitive to the destination node, and enters the Opened state. Upon receiving the OPN primitive, the destination node also enters the Opened state. The loop is now in a point-to-point configuration. Either of the open ports can now send command or data frames.

After completing the information exchange, the port that won arbitration sends a CLS primitive to the destination port. Both ports now return to the monitoring state.

3.16.4.2   The Monitoring State

After port initialization, all ports start in the monitoring state, the loop is idle, no data is being transmitted, and there is no activity. The loop at this time is considered to be closed. While in the monitoring state, ports act as repeaters and are looking for primitive signals and sequences to act upon. Before any port arbitrates for the loop, the loop is filled with Idles.

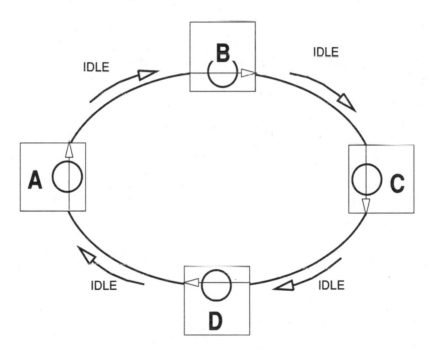

Figure 3-19   Monitoring or Idle State

3.16.4.3   The Arbitration Process

To begin the arbitration process, a port, in this example Port A, sends the primitive signal ARB(a) to notify the loop of its intention to own the loop. Port A wins arbitration when the ARB(a) is returned to it. Receiving its ARB(a) means no higher priority NL_Port needs the loop at this time.

When Port A wants to acquire the loop, there can be different conditions on the loop. For example:

- Some other port may already have control of the loop.

- Several ports may be trying to acquire the loop at the same time.

Port A will win when:

- No other port controls the loop, and

- No port with a lower AL_PA address (higher priority) is arbitrating.

Once a port has acquired the loop, it opens the loop, preventing all other ports from acquiring the loop. It receives and discards all ARB(x) primitive signals.

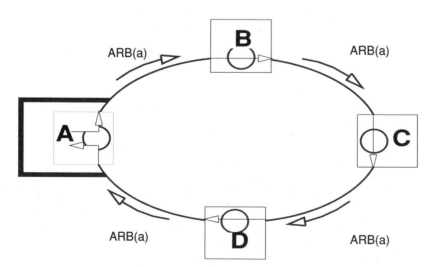

Figure 3-20   Arbitration Process

3.16.4.4   The Open State

In this example, Port A has acquired the loop. It is now in the Open state with the loop physically open at Port A. Nothing may be done until Port A has completed a circuit with its intended destination—in Figure 3-21, Port C.

Port A sends the OPN primitive signal naming C with an OPN(c,a) for full duplex or an OPN(c,c) for half duplex. Port C is monitoring the loop, acting as a repeater, and listening for any ordered set pertaining to it. Once it receives the OPN primitive signal from Port A, it enters the Open state and physically opens the loop at its port.

The loop is now open between Port A and C and is considered to be a point-to-point connection.

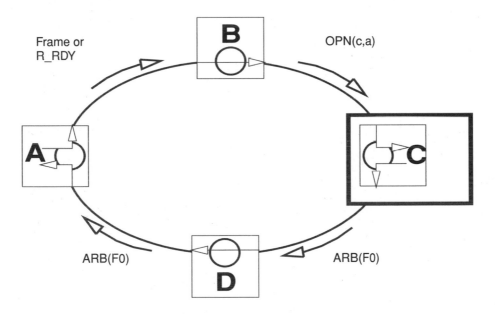

Figure 3-21   The Open State

3.16.4.5   Open Loop

Both Port A and Port C have opened the loop. Upper level protocol frames and link control frames may now be sent back and forth.

The circuit formed is essentially a point-to-point link between A and C. This is a dedicated path for the duration of the transaction.

Ports B and D are acting as repeaters, but are listening for specific ordered sets as before.

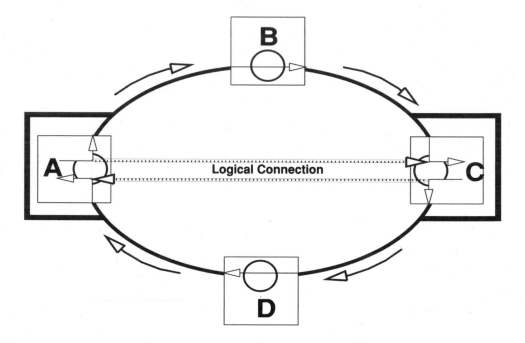

Figure 3-22   Open Loop

3.16.4.6   Closing the Loop

Either one of the Open ports may initiate the closing procedure by sending a CLS primitive signal to the other. In this example, Port A initiates the closing by sending the CLS signal.

Once a port has sent a CLS primitive signal, it may not send frames or R_RDYs. However, it may still receive frames and R_RDYs.

The port receiving the first CLS primitive signal—here, Port C—does not have to close its circuit right away. It may continue to send frames. Once its operation is complete, it sends a CLS primitive signal back to the other port, Port A.

Port C closes when it sends the CLS to Port A and Port A closes when it receives the CLS from Port C. The loop is now closed, with both ports returning to the monitoring state.

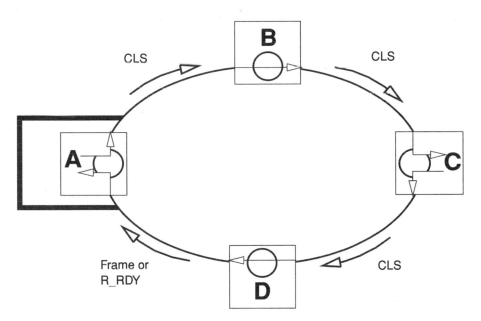

Figure 3-23   Closing the Loop

Once the loop is closed it returns to the monitoring or idle state shown in Figure 3-19. There is no activity and all nodes are retransmitting idle signals. When the loop is closed, other ports may acquire the loop.

Access fairness provides other ports on the loop have one chance to acquire the loop before the port that just owned the loop can acquire the loop again. Access fairness does not imply time fairness. In other words, a port may hold on to the loop as long as it is transmitting frames.

3.17 Hubs

FC_AL hubs connect devices to the loop. It is a simple way to connect participants in a private loop. There are two types of hubs:

- Passive, which only reacts to ports being inserted into or removed from a loop.
- Active, which are able to do configuration changes dynamically, based on some controlling protocol.

Some hubs can sense or manage configuration changes in the loop, including:

- knowing when NL_Ports are added

- knowing when NL_Ports are removed

- knowing when address changes occur for an entire set of NL_Ports

- switching NL_Ports into or out of a loop

Hubs also provide port bypass circuits to "heal" a loop when a device is removed or fails. This allows for less disruption in operations. Hubs help solve the problems of cabling devices and keeping track of which loop a device is on. With central cabling by way of the FC-AL hub, it is easy to add and remove devices from arbitrated loops.

There are some definite advantages to using Fibre Channel hub:

- Extremely fast solution for connecting peripherals and hosts (nodes)

- Up to 124 NL_Ports per loop

- Loop topology eliminates wiring clutter

- FC-AL hubs enhance subsystem availability

- FC-AL hubs provide port bypass circuits to permit "hot" repair

3.18 Hub Topologies

There will be more information about hubs in Chapter 4. For now, to demonstrate a couple of topologies using hubs see Figures 3-24 and 3-25.

3.18.1 Cascading Shortwave Hubs

A server with an FC-AL shortwave host bus adapter (HBA) can connect to an FC-AL hub 500 meters away. Each of the 10 ports on the hub can connect to an FC-AL device up to 500 meters away.

Cascaded hubs use one port on each hub for the hub-to-hub connection and this increases the potential distance between nodes in the loop an additional 500 meters. In this topology the overall distance is 1500m. Both hubs can support other FC-AL devices at their physical locations. Stated distances assume a 50 micron multimode cable.

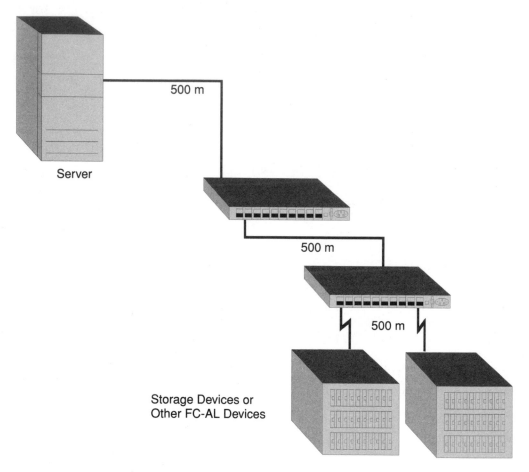

Figure 3-24   Cascaded Shortwave Hub Topology

3.18.2   Cascading Longwave Hubs

Cascaded FC-AL, non-OFC, longwave hubs use the long-wave port for the hub-to-hub connection. Ports 1 through 9 on each longwave hub are for connections to FC-AL devices. When cascading longwave hubs, only use the long-wave port on each hub to connect the hubs. The overall distance in this topology is 11,000 meters. There is 500 m from the server to the first hub, plus 10,000 m between the two longwave hubs, plus 500 m from the second hub to the final device.

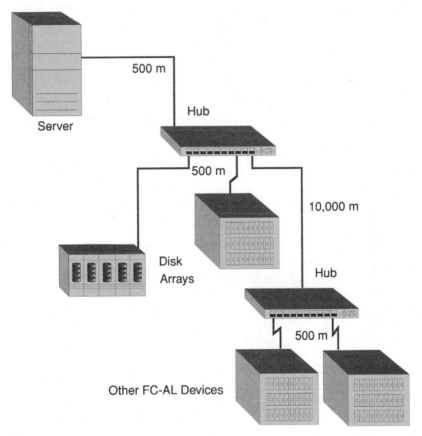

Figure 3-25   Cascaded Longwave Hub Topology

The SAN in Detail

This chapter discusses:

- **SAN principles**

- **SAN terms and building blocks**

- **SAN topologies**

- **Other SAN considerations**

In this chapter we build various SANs from the SAN building blocks.

4.1 SAN Principles

By creating a SAN from its component parts, we can see the promises and pitfalls in the topologies. As the components come together, certain practical connectivity considerations will assert themselves.

The old saying is, "In theory, there is no difference between theory and practice, but in practice there is." This is true of the SAN. The theoretical limits of capacity and performance have practical limitations. Some elements of connectivity do not yet work or don't work as well as they should.

Let's fabricate some SANs. We begin with principles and concepts we want to follow, and then describe some of the terms and building blocks that apply generally to all SAN building.

Then we'll create some topologies, building them up step by step. There are additional considerations besides the basic connections. Fault protection, distance, and tape backup topologies are among them.

We'll also look at legacy devices, and how to integrate them into the SAN. "Legacy" is a polite term for old equipment you already own and can't afford to replace. This is important, since most IT shops are not prepared to junk their older devices every time a new technology develops.

Once we've created some SANs, we'll look at SAN planning, maintenance, and management considerations. Finally, we'll wrap up with some SAN cost considerations.

4.1.1 Review of the Principles

We said in Chapter 1 that a SAN is an interconnected set of hardware devices. The SAN will exhibit most of these characteristics:

- Storage behind the server
- Storage devices connected to each other
- Multiple servers connected to the storage pool
- Heterogeneous servers may be connected to the storage pool
- Fibre Channel connectivity (FC host bus adapters and fiber optic cable)
- Hubs and switches
- Multiple paths to devices

Not all characteristics need be present. For example, some SANs don't have heterogeneous servers, as the enterprise has chosen a one-vendor server solution.

FC host bus adapters and fiber optic cable connections imply a full Fibre Channel interconnection, but that's not always possible. There's a need to connect SCSI devices to SANs. At this time, the majority of SANs back up data to SCSI tape libraries.

Some SANs don't have multiple paths to devices. These SANs operate at an elevated level of risk of failure, and we generally discourage that sort of connectivity. A foundation concept of the SAN is "no single point of failure," and most of our models in this chapter are built on that concept. Ideally, there should be at least two ways to get from one device to another.

SAN-building can be a gradual process. You can build the core SAN loop and migrate devices to it. Because of this, many data centers will have a combination of directly attached storage, Network Attached Storage, and SAN storage. However, as the benefits of the SAN assert themselves, the older storage connectivity options will fall by the wayside.

4.2 SAN Terms and Building Blocks

You should be familiar with the following components and their general capabilities before building the SAN.

4.2.1 Building Blocks

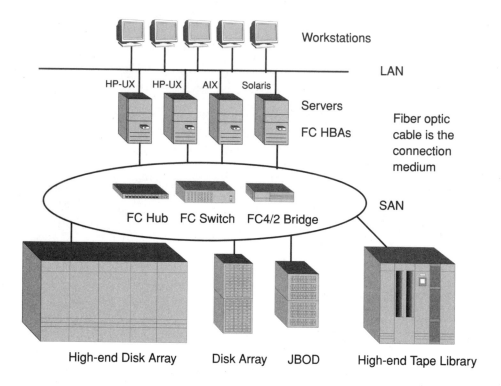

Figure 4-1   SAN Building Blocks

The top line of Figure 4-1 shows the workstations. They are connected to the LAN, as expected. The client view of stored data will not change in a SAN. The only expectation is that there should be some relief from storage bottlenecks, and data should be available when a SAN is used.

The next row is the servers, connected to the LAN, intended to run applications and deliver retrieved data to the client workstations. What's shown is a heterogeneous mix of open system (UNIX) servers.

Windows NT and IBM mainframes could just as easily appear in the illustration, although it would be reckless to say that interoperability concerns have been worked out. At the very least, heterogeneous servers can be connected to the SAN, and we are moving toward the day when each operating system better recognizes the file systems of the other operating systems.

Note that the servers have a single card in them, called a Fibre Channel Host Bus Adapter. In the balance of this chapter, you'll usually see two HBAs in each server, as multiple HBAs are an important part of fault-proofing a SAN.

The next row is the SAN, made up of various combinations of hubs, switches, and FC-SCSI bridges. The SAN is frequently represented as an ellipse (or a cloud, in the case of fabric-switched SANs). Whatever graphic is used, the idea is to broadly suggest an any-to-any connectivity of devices on the SAN. In fact, a Fibre Channel Arbitrated Loop (FC-AL) is really a loop. A switch is an any-to-any star topology. A bridge is a device that has both Fibre Channel and SCSI connections, allowing SCSI devices to be attached to the Fibre Channel network.

The SAN, of course, is the connection infrastructure between servers and storage devices. The connection medium is usually fiber optic cable, although connections over copper are permitted in the Fibre Channel standards, and some copper-based devices are available.

At the bottom are the storage devices. The typical primary storage device on a SAN is the high-availability disk array. However, the JBOD (just a bunch of disks) is still with us. The JBOD is commonly a collection of SCSI disks in an enclosure, but Fibre Channel JBODs are available, too. The JBOD "disk farm" or "disk hotel" is still useful for meeting some data center needs.

The typical secondary storage device is the tape library. Although single-mechanism tape drives and autochangers can be part of a SAN, the basic assumption is that the SAN is a topology for massive disk storage, and massive disk storage needs massive tape backup.

Magneto Optical devices certainly can appear on a SAN, and they fill the need for online delivery of archival or reference data (usually on read-only media). MO isn't discussed in this chapter. However, in Chapter 6, we consider re-writable MO as a possible backup medium.

4.2.2 Capabilities

SAN components form something like a high-tech Lego set, so in order to build a SAN, we should be familiar with what each piece can do.

As stated in the preface, we use HP equipment in our examples. This is not an infomercial for HP, which we leave to HP's product briefs and Web site. It is simply because we are most familiar with this equipment and have worked on the teams that developed the products. HP products are excellent; however, be aware that other manufacturers make products that will work fine on a SAN, and HP has announced its commitment to an open SAN technology.

Fiber optic cable capabilities.   That's not a spelling error. *Fibre* Channel uses *fiber* optic cable. The fiber optic cable may be 9 micron single mode, and can be used for distances of up to 10 km. The cable may be 50 micron multi-mode (distances to 500 meters) or 62.5 micron multimode (distances to 375 meters). Incidentally, Fibre Channel is also supported over copper connections.

Hub capabilities.   HP's two Fibre Channel hub offerings are good models for hubs in general. The shortwave hub (called the HP SureStore E Hub S10) has ten ports. It can be cascaded into one other longwave or shortwave hub. The shortwave hub is the right hub for installations covering short distances, using 50 or 62.5 micron cable.

The longwave hub (the HP SureStore E Hub L10) has 10 ports. It can be cascaded into one other longwave or shortwave hub. The longwave hub is the right one for distance requirements of up to 10 km, using 9 micron cable.

Bridge capabilities.   The HP FC4/2 Bridge has two Fibre Channel ports for connection to the SAN. It has four SCSI ports for connection to SCSI devices.

Switch capabilities. Hewlett-Packard configurations use the Brocade 2800 switch. It is a 16-port fabric switch with the capability of cascading or meshing switches into very large fabrics.

Disk array capabilities. A typical disk array is Fibre Channel-enabled, and provides substantial storage capacity. The high-availability features of a disk array are hot-swappable fans, power supplies, controllers, and disk drives. Battery backup for cache memory is another useful high-availability feature. These arrays are usually RAID-enabled. We base our SAN models on the HP Sure-Store E Disk Array FC60. It's a high-end product, offering about 1.6 TB of storage in a fully-populated 2.0 meter rack. The largest deployed HP disk array is the XP256, with a capacity of about 12 TB. The XP512 has just been announced.

JBOD capabilities. JBODs are still with us, in both SCSI and Fibre Channel versions. The HP FC 10 as a Fibre Channel JBOD. The HP SureStore E Disk System SC10, a SCSI JBOD, is a good candidate for a SAN. It has ten 9 GB or 18 GB drives for a maximum capacity of 180 GB per enclosure. Also, each device takes up only 3.5 EIA rack units, so you can rackmount up to ten of them in a rack, yielding 1.8 TB. The high-availability features of a modern JBOD are hot-swappable fans, power supplies, bus control cards, and disk drives.

4.2.3 Failure Proofing

There are a number of terms related to minimizing the impact of component failure in storage devices. These include "high availability," "fault tolerant," "self-healing," "redundancy," etc.

Since RAID technology reduced the impact of lost data in terms of a disk failure, it was only natural that disk array designers turned to other parts of the box that could fail. In particular, controller, fan, and power supply failures could make the device unavailable, making the data unavailable. The answer was simple enough: put two or more of each item in the device.

The point of redundant components is, of course, to allow the device to keep working until the defective part can be replaced. The functionality of the box is "self-healing," although unfortunately the broken part is not. Service personnel still have to replace it.

There are event monitoring and alerting capabilities in almost every component on a SAN, to alert you to component failures. One useful advancement in high-end devices is the "phone home" capability, found in the HP SureStore E Disk Array XP256. When the disk array senses a failure, it contacts HP service so immediate action can be taken.

Even HBAs report failures as "events," and their onboard LEDs are also a good indicator that something is wrong. The more recent HBAs have customer-replaceable GBICs, so it's not difficult to keep the HBAs operating.

Hubs shut down failed ports, and as hub management software improves, hub problems become easier to isolate and fix. Keeping the data flowing without interruption is due to providing multiple paths that go around failed hubs.

Multiple paths to a device is an important concept in a SAN. And it's easier to ensure multiple pathing in a SAN than it is in a arrangement of SCSI mass storage devices.

Even defective fiber optic cable can be overcome as a problem. Inside a data center, a bad crimp in the fiber cable bend can ruin its ability to carry data. In cross-campus cable link, the landscaper's backhoe can sever a cable. But if the cable runs are well worked out, these problems can be avoided, and because of dual pathing, data flows should not be interrupted.

The operative concept is "no single point of failure." If any component fails, there is another component that instantly takes its place until the defective part is replaced.

Assumptions about power.   Take care of your power. Even the best planned SAN is susceptible to power outages. The uninterruptible power supply (UPS) or standby generator can be your best friend. It also helps to have a reliable power company.

If an earthquake or hurricane strikes, your data center will probably lose power. However, at that point, a power loss (and loss of data) will not be your biggest worry. The good news is that, with the most durable SANs, you will have made a mirror image copy of your data, made as little as ten minutes before the catastrophe, and it's resident on your company's disaster recovery SAN, located many kilometers away.

4.3 SAN Topologies

For the development of SAN topologies, we won't show the workstations or the LAN in the illustrations.

4.3.1 Working Up to a SAN

Let's begin with a fundamental Fibre Channel connection.

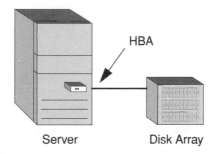

Figure 4-2   A Simple Point-to-point Connection

This is a simple point-to-point connection, with one server and one disk array. Now a point-to-point connection isn't much to write home about. It is not quite a SAN, but it is a useful server/storage connection.

Our connection is fast, and more convenient to cable than a SCSI connection, but it isn't very reliable. The single points of failure are: server, FC HBA, cable, disk array controller. So, we'll add some additional connectivity.

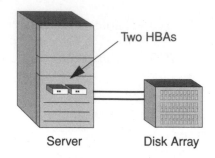

Server   Disk Array

Figure 4-3   A Point-to-point Connection with Two Paths

Here's the connection with a second FC HBA in the server and a cable path to the disk array's second controller.

If either FC HBA, cable, or disk array controller fails, there's still a path between the server and the disk array.

The single point of failure is the server. Since a server failure is possible, let's add another server.

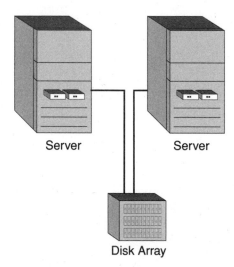

Server   Server

Disk Array

Figure 4-4   Point-to-point Connections from Two Servers

Here, each server connects to a disk array controller.

This isn't going to work for us. In fact, it has made matters worse. The single points of failure are:

* Server 1: server, FC HBA, cable, disk array controller

* Server 2: server, FC HBA, cable, disk array controller

If any part of the Server 1 chain fails, the whole chain goes down. The same is true of Server 2. The best case is that if one chain fails, the other chain should operate.

Another limitation is that this disk array only has two Fibre Channel ports, one for each controller. Other disk arrays, with more connections, could cross connect to both servers. Let's improve the arrangement.

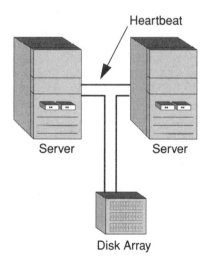

Figure 4-5 Clustered Servers

Here's a server cluster. If one server goes down, the other one will continue to deliver the applications.

The single points of failure are:

* Server 1: FC HBA, cable, disk array controller

* Server 2: FC HBA, cable, disk array controller

Now, let's add the rest of the equipment.

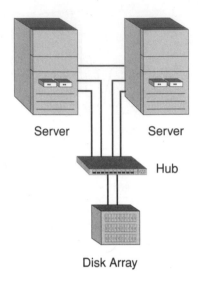

Figure 4-6 Fibre Channel Arbitrated Loop

The "rest of the equipment" is simply a hub. When we add a hub, we no longer have point-to-point connections. We have a Fiber Channel Arbitrated Loop (FC-AL). At this point, its not a complex loop at all, but this is just a starting point.

Each server connects to the hub on two paths from two HBAs. Each disk array controller connects to the hub. Now there are multiple continuous paths from each server to each disk array controller.

The single point of failure is the hub, so let's add another hub.

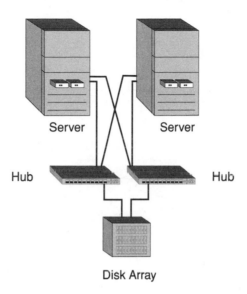

Figure 4-7 FC-AL with Two Hubs

When we add a second hub, we have a configuration that is now a fully-expandable SAN.

The clustered servers connect to each hub on two paths from separate HBAs. Each disk array controller connects to a hub. Now there are no single points of failure.

Because of the addition of the second hub, we are now free to experiment with scalability and distance.

4.3.1.1   Scalability

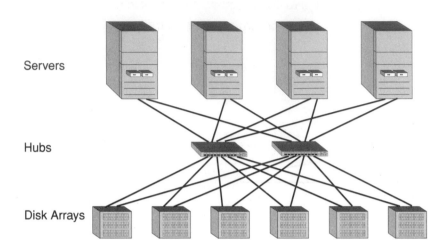

Figure 4-8 · FC-AL with Two Hubs and Ten Devices

The hubs used in these illustrations have ten ports each. How will we fill them? We should not consider one server and nine disk arrays, because that would make the server the single point of failure.

This is not true of an arrangement with nine servers and one disk array, since a high availability disk array has several redundant components. This is reflected later in this section, when we use a high-end disk array, which (to quote the user documentation) "is not expected to fail in any way."

In the above illustration, one port on each hub is used by each of the four servers. That leaves room on each hub for six storage devices.

The above six storage devices could each represent over 1 TB of stored data, so this as not a minor SAN.

Multiple paths are in place and there is no single point of failure.

4.3.1.2 Distance

You can use Fibre Channel to locate components much farther apart than with SCSI, which typically permits maximum cable lengths of 25 meters.

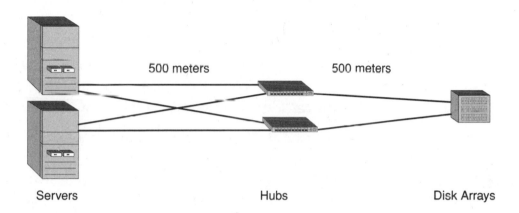

Figure 4-9   FC-AL at Maximum Distance

This is merely Figure 4-7 stretched across the building. In theory, we can locate the hub about 500 meters from the server, and locate the disk array another 500 meters from the hub. In discussions of 10 km distances over 9 micron cable, this "extra kilometer" is often forgotten.

In reality, the hubs would be located very near the servers or the storage devices. So a better way to achieve distance using hubs is to cascade the hubs.

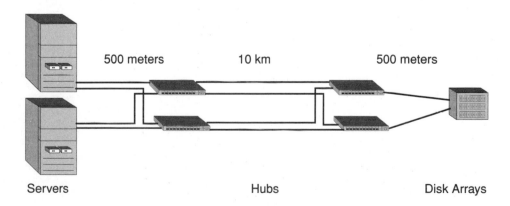

Figure 4-10   FC-AL with Cascaded Hubs

With cascaded longwave hubs, the fiber cable distance limit is 10 km. This makes virtually any on-campus SAN topology possible. You are limited only by the complexities of laying the fiber cable between buildings.

There are risks in using hubs in longer distance cable runs. Those risks can include a degradation in access time and some loss of received optical power. In Figure 4-10, there will be a propagation delay of 50 ms for data traveling in each direction, for a total of 100 ms. This is the equivalent of a loss of 1 MBps. In terms of power loss, the received optical power must be more positive (less than -17dBm) at the target, and you can test for this using an optical power meter.

What is illustrated is theoretically possible, but we would not recommend hubs as the first choice for solving distance problems. Since FC-AL is a loop topology, every device on the loop would feel the effects of the degradation caused by even one distant device. There can also be significant performance losses due to arbitration time and the lack of buffering.

When a configuration calls for distance, the fabric switch is the preferred choice.

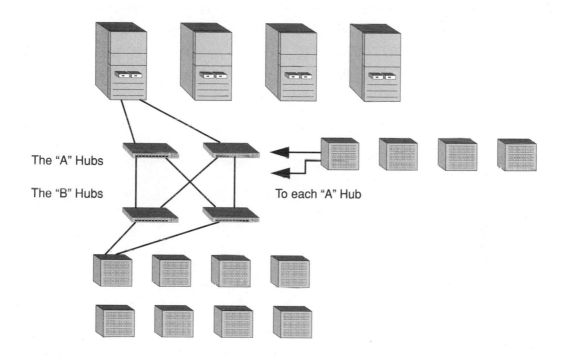

The "A" Hubs

The "B" Hubs   To each "A" Hub

Figure 4-11 FC-AL, Cascaded Hubs and Full Buildout

In Figure 4-11, not all connections are illustrated.

Here, cascaded 10-port hubs connect to each another. The cascading requires two ports on each of the "A" hubs to reach the "B" hubs, leaving eight ports on each hub. Those ports can connect to eight devices over dual paths.

The cascading also takes two ports on each of the "B" hubs, leaving eight ports on each hub. Those ports can connect to eight devices over dual paths

Those 16 ports can be any combination of FC devices. Here we've shown four servers and 12 disk arrays, but it could be eight servers and eight arrays.

How can you connect 16 servers? Use four "A" hubs, and two "B" hubs, and you'll be able to hook up two disk arrays to the resulting FC-AL.

The advantages and disadvantages of longer distances between devices is still present in the Figure 4-11. Devices linked over a distance impose a penalty in time on the entire loop. This occurs in two ways: First, I/O between server and storage device takes slightly longer because of distance; and second, when devices are arbitrating for use of the loop, the ARB primitives must circulate throughout the entire set of loop connections.

Let's use a Fibre Channel switch instead.

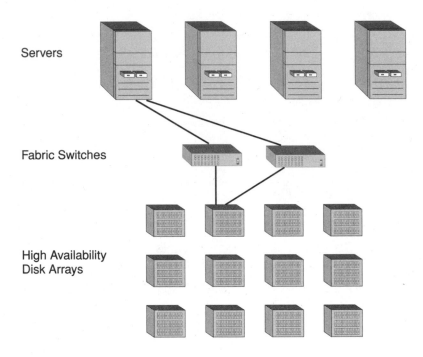

Figure 4-12 SAN with Fabric Switches

In Figure 4-12, not all connections are illustrated.

This is a 16-port switch and will establish dual-pathed, switched connections between any two of the devices.

A good switch has multiple fans in a module, dual power supplies and individual replaceable GBICs on the ports. However, it's still valuable to run separate paths through two switches. So the above illustration shows two paths from each server to each switch and two paths from each switch to each disk array.

A switch currently costs about four times as much as a hub, so why would you want to consider it? The following table, drawn from HP's switch training for customer engineers, compares hubs and switches.

Table 4-1   Hubs and Switches Compared

Hub	Switch
Moderate equipment cost – excellent entry-level implementation	Higher equipment cost offset by lower cost of ownership with management services
Small systems – limited connectivity (up to 126) with a single loop	Medium to large systems – increased connectivity with multiple switches
Shared media – single communication at a time	Unshared media – multiple concurrent communications
Limited performance – latency and throughput	Highest performance – latency and throughput
No isolation between a single device from the rest of loop's devices	Point-to-point link with the switch provides isolation between one device and the other devices
Single point of failure with one power cord	Dual power supplies with dual power cords avoids single point of failure

It may be true that "Higher equipment cost [is] offset by lower cost of ownership with management services," but you'll have to determine your Total Cost of Ownership (TCO) by the formulas that prevail in your operation.

Also take it with a grain of salt that smaller systems use hubs while larger systems use switches. There is a place for both devices in both small and large systems. And, in reference to "Dual power supplies and dual power cords avoids [sic] single point of failure," it's still important to maintain multiple paths between devices, whether you use hubs or switches.

Fabric switches are undoubtedly the wave of the future, but there will always be a place for the FC-AL hub. To illustrate this, let's attach some hubs to switches.

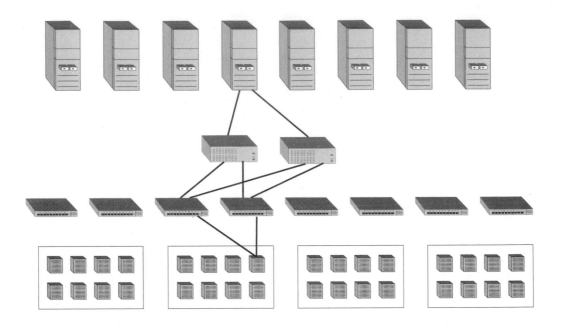

Figure 4-13   SAN with Switches and Hubs

In Figure 4-13, not all connections are illustrated.

The servers are connected to the switches over multiple paths. The switches connect to each hub over multiple paths, and the disk arrays connect to the hubs over multiple paths.

Considering that each disk array could be an FC60 or equivalent, this storage pool could contain 32 devices with a capacity of about 1.6 TB each. That would be a total of 51.2 TB.

If we were to "pool" the servers using hubs, it might look like this:

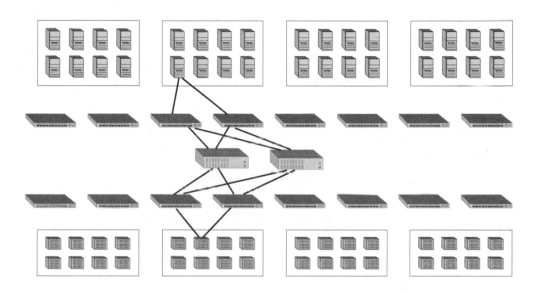

Figure 4-14 SAN with Server Pools and Storage Pools

In Figure 4-14, not all connections are illustrated.

Scalability like this is possible, and it can be done with hubs. However, since switches like the Brocade Silkworm 2800 are certified to cascade up to 32 switches over seven hops, it would be better to consider switches for such a complex arrangement of devices.

There are a lot of storage devices illustrated above. However, a single large disk array might be easier to manage. It would certainly take up a good deal less floor space.

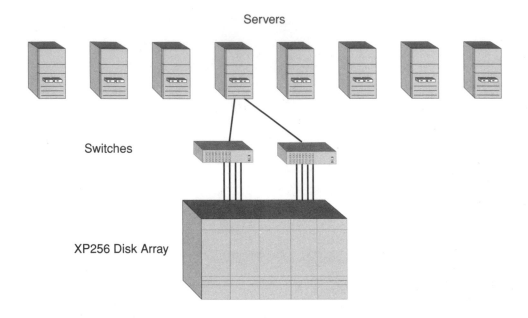

Figure 4-15   Connecting to a High-end Disk Array

In Figure 4-15, not all connections are illustrated.

In the arrangement illustrated above, eight Fibre Channel ports on the disk array are used. When connected with switches, a large number of devices on the SAN gain access to the disk array at full bandwidth.

There are up to 256 disk drives in one XP256, and it has a relatively small footprint. Given HP's current maximum capacity point of 47 GB, that gives the XP256 a capacity of about 12 TB. If you put eight of these on the floor of your data center, you are very close to one petabyte of mass storage.

This disk array has 1024 LUNs, and management software allows you to make smaller ones (using CVS, or Custom Volume Size) or larger ones (using LUSE, or Logical Unit Size Expansion). The Cache LUN feature puts LUN contents into RAM, which helps data to move at much faster speeds.

4.3.2 Building from Legacy Equipment

But what, you may say, can I do with my legacy equipment? Use it on the SAN. Despite falling per-gigabyte costs for new native Fibre Channel storage hardware, legacy storage is still valuable, and worth keeping. It's expensive, often acquired one piece at a time, and must stay in service as long as possible. Legacy equipment is commonly SCSI equipment.

Very few data centers transitioning to a SAN would buy all new Fibre Channel devices and make a wholesale conversion. As you build your SAN and it grows stable, you are likely to bring SCSI equipment on to the SAN a few devices at a time. Additionally, "the show must go on," so you need to keep running your legacy equipment while the SAN is developing.

SCSI equipment that you will transition would include:

- High-availability (HA) SCSI disk arrays

- SCSI JBODs

- SCSI tape libraries

- SCSI single-mech tape drives or autochangers

Here's where the FC4/2 bridge comes in. The bridge has two Fibre Channel ports and four SCSI ports.

You can connect the bridge to Fibre Channel hubs or switches. One caution here, however. SCSI Tape drives do not do well when they share a hub with other citizens of a Fiber Channel Arbitrated Loop. Here's a quote from the product literature for the FC4/2 bridge:

> In a dynamic environment such as a Fibre Channel Arbitrated Loop, availability of devices—reserving a Fibre Channel tape device on a SAN, for example—can be a concern. A tape backup in progress can be interrupted by the dynamics of the FC-AL (e.g., a LIP occurs when a server is power cycled). Error handling in the backup application needs close attention to ensure that data loss does not occur and that the chance of a failed command is recoverable.

Even HP's top of the line tape library, the SureStore E 20/700, is SAN-enabled only by means of an FC4/2 bridge.

Anyway, let's bring some SCSI devices onto the SAN.

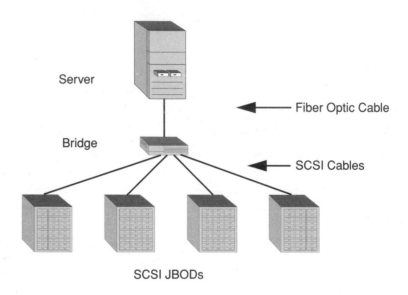

Figure 4-16   Using a Bridge to Connect SCSI Devices

Here's a simple entry into the world of Fibre Channel. One server is connected to one bridge, and the bridge is connected to four SCSI disk enclosures.

The single points of failure are the server, the HBA, the bridge, and the JBOD—just about everything.

An improvement might be to connect a second server to the bridge's other Fibre Channel port. Alternately, connecting a second fiber cable from the server to the bridge would be a small improvement. But overall, this arrangement does not display the kind of reliability we'd like to see.

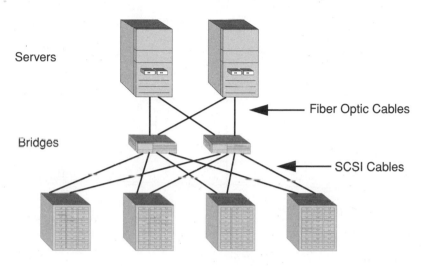

Servers

Fiber Optic Cables

Bridges

SCSI Cables

High Availability SCSI Disk Systems (HP SC10s)

Figure 4-17   Two Bridges and HA SCSI Disk Systems

Here, two servers are crossconnected to two bridges. To those bridges, we can connect modern SCSI disk systems, which have some high-availability components. In particular, dual controllers in some SCSI disk arrays permit connection to two switches.

Now, there is no single point of failure.

4.3.2.1   Device Mix

To bring other SCSI devices onto a SAN, we can build on the topology illustrated in Figure 4-17.

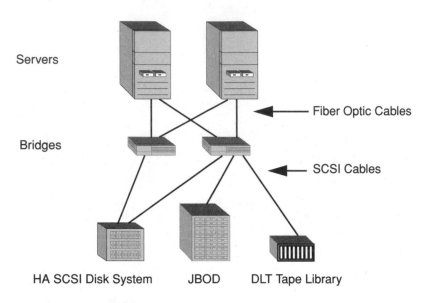

Figure 4-18   A Mix of SCSI Devices

Unlike hubs, bridges should not present problems with mixing devices (Figure 4-18). We continue to employ two bridges so the high-availability SCSI disk system has some failure proofing. In this example, the legacy JBOD and DLT tape library only have one SCSI port and cannot be double-pathed to the bridges.

The arrangement leaves open ports on the bridges, and would permit four more connections.

4.3.2.2 Capacity

Let's make the bridges citizens in a fabric by attaching them to switches. By attaching a larger number of bridges, and we'll be able to attach many SCSI devices.

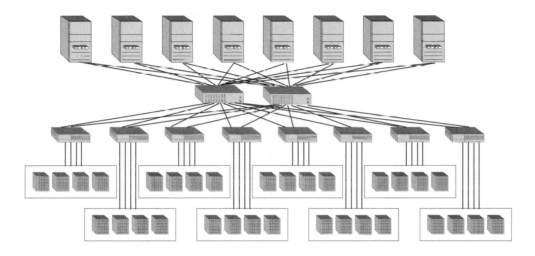

Figure 4-19   Connecting a Lot of JBODs

Here's an arrangement of servers, non-cascaded switches, bridges and JBODs. Every available port is filled.

The switches allow us to attach 16 devices, in this case eight servers and eight FC4/2 bridges. All the items are double pathed, with the exception of the JBODs. With high-availability SCSI disk systems, we'd cut the number of devices in half, but they would be double pathed to the bridges.

The same arrangement can be accomplished with hubs instead of bridges, but the number of connections available on the hubs would be ten.

4.3.3 Adding Tape

How do we go about adding a SCSI tape library? There are two considerations: first, we'll need to use a FC4/2 bridge; second, we don't want to mix disk and tape I/O on a hub.

Let's begin by adding a tape library directly attached to a server.

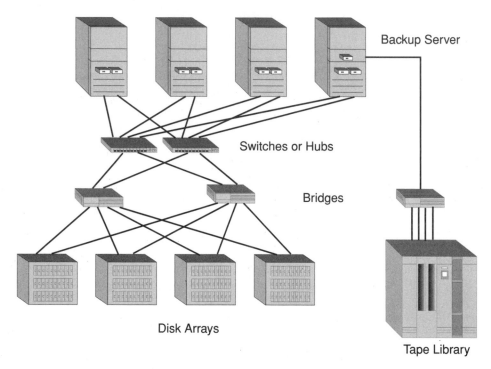

Figure 4-20   Adding a SCSI-based Tape Library

In this arrangement, we revisit our four-server setup with its connection through bridges to four high-availability SCSI disk systems. Of course, the disk units could just as easily be Fibre Channel high-availability disk arrays.

To build a dedicated path for the tape, we add another Fiber Channel HBA to one of the servers. That is connected to a bridge connected to the tape library. We've designated this server as the backup server.

In this example, the single point of failure is connection from the server's single HBA to the single bridge. We could add an HBA to another server and cross-connect them through two hubs to two bridges. That would provide dou-ble-pathing.

4.3.4 Backup Over the SAN

The following illustrates compact and typical large scale configuration: high-end disk arrays and tape backup through a bridge.

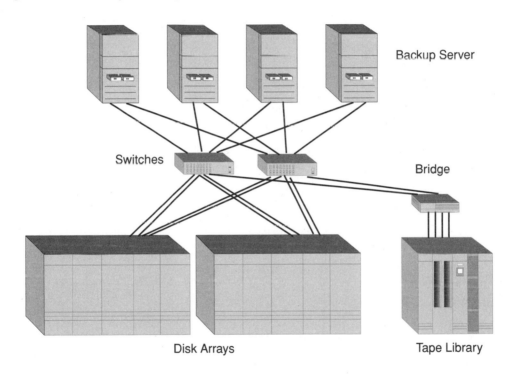

Figure 4-21   Backup Over the SAN

Here, a switch is a compact method of improving connectivity. A bridge is still required by the tape drive, but it can be connected to both switches.

If the tape library has high-available features, the single point of failure is the bridge. With a Fibre Channel-ready tape library, we can eliminate the bridge.

In a SAN equipped with the correct hardware and backup software, the "LAN-free" or "serverless" backup is possible.

4.3.5 The Next Step in the SAN

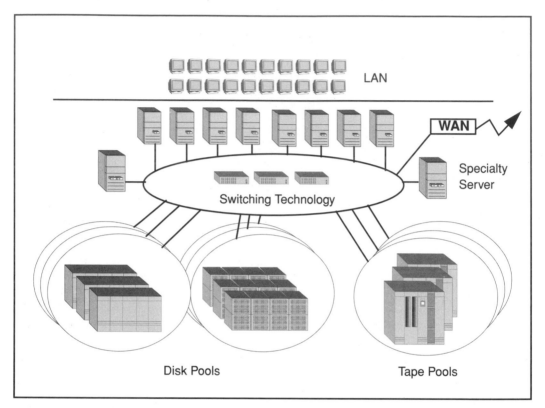

Figure 4-22   SAN Evolution

As the SAN evolves, we are beginning to see sophisticated switching capabilities. Combine that with the current announcement of 2 GB Fibre Channel and the plans for 4 GB Fibre Channel and there should be plenty of speed and connectivity options.

As a result, look for vast disk pools and tape pools, with full bandwidth connectivity. The storage pools need not be located near the servers or each other.

Look for specialty servers, such as database servers, data movement servers, backup servers, and SAN management servers.

4.4 Other SAN Considerations

A SAN is not difficult to configure and implement. However, managing and maintaining a SAN can be a challenge, primarily because of growth and complexity.

As the number of devices on the SAN grows linearly, the number of potential interactions increases. This is a good thing for bringing storage to servers and clients, but it could create management headaches.

The most successful SAN implementation will reflect planning, good management, and a sense of the cost/value proposition the SAN offers.

4.4.1 Planning

If you are thinking of implementing a SAN, you'll find that the planning is your first ally. There is a lot of order at the heart of the SAN, and if you plan carefully, you'll be able to buy, implement, and manage SAN equipment with fewer problems.

If you work in a chaos-driven topsy-turvy shop, as many of us have, the conversion to a SAN gives you a chance to imprint some order on a somewhat out-of-control storage topology. Your SCSI arrangement may have gotten a little out of hand, and with the SAN, you'll be off to a fresh start.

A planning document is the blueprint for SAN success. At its most complex, it can show every device and device address. At the very least, it demonstrates to management your plan for an orderly implementation. Whether you create a one-page or 100-page document as a blueprint for your SAN, create something. Ask yourself (and answer) the following questions:

- **Current configuration.** What equipment do I have now? How much legacy equipment can I work into a new SAN?

- **Current needs.** What's working well in my current configuration? What are the performance and connectivity shortfalls in the current implementation?

- **Future needs.** What are my expansion plans for servers, storage, wide area interconnections, etc?

- **Rate of storage growth.** How fast is storage growing now? When will I run out? At what rate in the future will I be scaling up storage?

- **Budget.** What does new equipment cost? What does it get me? Can I justify this to management?

- **Topology.** What will the new SAN look like? Where will I locate the equipment? What about cabling runs?

- **Management.** How will I monitor and manage my SAN? How will I tune performance?

- **Intangibles.** Will I be able to do more with greater ease? Will I be able to manage storage with fewer worries?

A good SAN plan can get your implementation started. It's also easier to expand a well-planned SAN. If you can, keep your SAN plan up to date.

4.4.2 SAN Management and Maintenance

A SAN is easier to maintain and manage than a SCSI storage configuration. Certainly, when equipment is stable and performing as expected, there is very little to manage.

SAN maintenance is primarily hardware maintenance. The device is either broken or it's not. However, with the SAN, you have enough failure-proofing to eliminate many downtime headaches while locating broken equipment.

HP has a set of tools for monitoring the status of the SAN. They are essentially device management tools, intended to check specifically if an HBA, a hub, a switch or a bridge is performing.

At a minimum, management tools should allow you to:

- Monitor the overall status of all supported devices on the Storage Area Network

- Monitor the operational status of each supported device (fans, power supply, and temperature)

- Determine which switch, hub, and bridge ports are in use

- Bypass and enable switch and hub ports

- View switch information, such as: topology, status errors, statistics and performance

HP's SAN Manager Device Manager (DM) and SAN Manager Lun Manager (LM) are comprehensive SAN management packages. SAN Manager DM focuses on device management. SAN Manager LM is an efficient way to manage, assign and secure storage resources.

Performance management is also important. After spending money and time to put together a SAN, the last thing you want to hear is that "the network runs slow." Fortunately, performance tuning software is getting better. If you happen to buy an XP256, there is the optional software package, Performance Manager XP, which allows for easy performance measurement and easy parameter changes.

4.4.3 Cost Factors

Marketing literature from hardware manufacturers consistently cites a lower "Total Cost of Ownership (TCO)" as a SAN selling point. However, the mathematics of TCO is never spelled out.

It is expected that the cost of buying relatively expensive new equipment is mitigated by reduced maintenance costs and some measurable performance boosts. Unfortunately, the device is usually not shipped with a cost accountant in the accessory box to help you calculate the TCO.

Here are some of the SAN TCO factors.

4.4.3.1 Tangibles

- **Old cable runs will save money.** If you have FDDI 62.5 micron cable in place, you can use it to connect shortwave hubs without recabling. This can save some money.

- **New cable runs will cost money.** However, fiber optic cable is relatively cheap, and the increased distances permitted by Fibre Channel make it easier to plan cable runs. The labor to "pull cable" is not cheap; however, fiber is relatively easy to route and there may be cabling jobs in the data center you can do without hiring outside vendors.

- **No more SCSI cables.** You won't need to buy more of those fat, costly cables. That's money back into the budget.

- **Hubs, switches, and bridges will cost money.** Yes, but the hubs are a relatively low-cost item, and you can get a lot of mileage out of them. However, be prepared to buy switches, as the switched fabric has connectivity and performance advantages you will need in the future.

- **Legacy SCSI storage devices will save money.** There's tread life left on those SCSI JBODs—those you bought last year and those you bought last week. For the price of an FC4/2 bridge, they can join the SAN. You'll have to determine how long you might be able to use them before you abandon them in favor of Fibre Channel-enabled storage devices.

- **Fibre Channel storage devices will cost money.** You'll have to check each product individually, but generally when you look at the capabilities of a Fibre Channel storage device, there's a good value proposition. The capacities are high, with a generally good GB/dollar ratio. Expandability and reliability are worth something, too. For many installations, they are worth a lot.

4.4.3.2 Intangibles

Intangibles have value, although they are sometimes difficult to measure. For example, in selling a business, "good will" is an intangible, yet the seller of a business must assign a monetary value to it. With a SAN, there are intangible cost factors, as well.

What is the worth of satisfied users, satisfied customers, satisfied management? In particular, technology that satisfies customers enhances the enterprise. As a personal matter, IT management's satisfaction with storage management will certainly be important to you during your annual review.

And what's the worth of your worrying less and feeling better about storage problems? A SAN will lower the Total Cost of Frustration (TCF) and the Total Cost of Headaches (TCH).

- **Distance runs get easier.** That SCSI distance limitation, across the room or across the campus, is eliminated. SCSI cabling, with a nominal maximum length of 25 meters (or 75 meters with a booster/expander), cannot compete. This is even more true if you consider the TCF of handling thick SCSI cable.

- **Intrarack cabling gets easier.** If you've ever tried to populate a 2.0 meter rack with 16 dual-ported SCSI JBODs installed back-to-back, you know what we mean. The cabling is impossible. Fibre Channel is much easier and this saves on your labor, CE labor, and TCF/TCH.

- **HBA maintenance gets easier.** A Fibre Channel HBA GBIC is a Customer Replaceable Unit (CRU) in some devices. There's a labor, time, and frustration savings here.

- **Scaling gets easier.** That SAN planning you did will pay off when you scale up the SAN. You'll essentially just plug a new device into a hub or switch, and there you are! Of course, there's a little more to it than that, but it's relatively easy. And you're not just installing one device for one server. You've added a device to the SAN that's potentially available to all devices on the SAN.

- **Backups get harder.** Since storage is easy to add, you will add it. New storage capacity always makes backups longer (and of course slower). However, there are some great workarounds. These are discussed in Chapter 6.

- **Management and maintenance get easier.** Hard to believe, but you will be able to manage more devices with less effort without getting out of your chair. Of course, there will be times when you'll have to go to the back of a server to look at the Fault LED on an HBA, but you'll get your first indication of trouble at your workstation.

- **Reliability pays off.** Inevitably, there will be broken equipment, but with the SAN you should see few broken paths. The enterprise saves valuable time and money, because the impact of a down system is largely eliminated. This should save you any headaches created by working through crises.

4.5 Summary

The operating premise that today's IT environment serves up information to users and customers 100% of the time is becoming 100% true.

SCSI's direct connection of servers and storage isn't sufficient to provide the availability, flexibility, performance, scalability, and fault tolerance now required. The SAN topology delivers.

CHAPTER 5

Managing the SAN

This chapter discusses:

- **Generic requirements for SAN management**
- **SAN Manager LUN Management (LM)**
- **SAN Manager Device Management (DM)**

*The best SAN is a well-managed SAN. This chapter describes HP manage-
ment and monitoring software for SANs.*

5.1   Generic Requirements for SAN Management

After the SAN has been designed and built, the administrator will need to be able to manage all the equipment now associated with the SAN. There are three major areas of management that need to be considered:

- controlling
- monitoring
- servicing

Control in the sense of SAN management refers to the ability to modify the state of the SAN resources. For example:

- configuring a disk array
- assigning LUN associations
- setting levels of security

SAN management control must be able to provide heterogeneous node support. Storage products used in today's networking environments are likely to be from different manufacturers, but must work together on the SAN. One of the purposes of the SAN, after all, is to pool resources in order to reduce expenses and confusion.

The control portion of SAN management must also provide a single system image. The administrator must be able to view and modify all devices connected within the SAN from a single point. This would include devices such as:

- storage devices
  - disks
  - tapes
- servers
  - UNIX
  - NT
- infrastructure components
  - hubs
  - switches

Having a single point of control also provides for better security of the management of the SAN. And finally, the addition and removal of nodes to the SAN should be accomplished without disruption to the network.

Monitoring is the ability to observe the state of the SAN. This would include the ability to understand the relationships between:

- storage subsystems
- server nodes
- fabrics
- allocations of assets within the network

As with control, monitoring requires the ability to see the entire SAN in order to inventory hardware and to view and manage capacity, use, and performance. Monitoring is a nondestructive activity, and therefore typically doesn't require as high a level of security as the control function. Monitoring should also provide a centralized capability. Centralized monitoring is essential for managing a large SAN extended over many kilometers or across campuses.

Service refers to the activities of:

- finding and resolving problems
- performing preventive maintenance

For example, servicing a SAN requires the ability to diagnose hardware problems on components within the SAN without interfering extensively with throughput. Also, adding and removing nodes should be accomplished without disrupting the SAN. This means that not only should the troubleshooting procedures be transparent to the user, but the design of the storage network should support the removal and replacement of components without interrupting data flow.

5.2   Hewlett-Packard SAN Management Products

HP announced in April, 2000, that it supports and is committed to an open Storage Area Network standard. The HP approach is called the HP Equation storage architecture.

This vision is of an open, virtual pool of storage devices that efficiently offer 100% data availability, flexibility, and scalability. This result should be a "storage grid," analogous to the electrical power grid.

5.2.1   Overview of Two SAN Management Products

Hewlett-Packard's SAN Manager LM (LUN Management) and SAN Manager DM (Device Management) products are very recent offerings. They are good examples of the kind of software needed to manage storage on the SAN. They are both supported on HP-UX, NT, and Solaris hosts.

SAN Manager LM enables LUNs in the storage pool to be assigned through a drag-and-drop interface and secures the assignments by making them visible to only the associated server. It works in a heterogeneous server/storage environment.

SAN Manager DM is a real-time SAN monitor. It provides a physical view and a centralized platform to manage configuration changes. It is a critical element in defining topology and establishing a means to physically control the SAN.

Through additional plug-ins, HP says it will provide LUN mirroring, performance monitoring, SAN backup, capacity management, remote diagnosis, and many other storage management capabilities. As that becomes true, SAN Manager DM should be an effective SAN management solution.

5.2.2 SAN Manager LUN Management (LM)

HP SureStore E SAN Manager LUN Management (LM) software is a server-based SAN management solution. It provides SAN storage access control. It's an efficient way to build and manage complex server/storage security assignments. You assign storage access to some hosts and exclude other hosts from access.

SAN Manager LM runs in a heterogeneous server/storage environment. Storage from various manufacturers can be treated as a pool of devices that can be assigned to any host.

5.2.2.1 Ease of Use

During installation, SAN Manager LM automatically discovers all the storage devices and hosts on the SAN. As a result, very little information has to be entered manually.

The Device Group feature is used to organize storage devices into logical groups, making it easy to locate and assign devices. To assign storage, you select individual devices or an entire Device Group with the mouse and drag it to a host. Storage assigned exclusively to each host is clearly displayed in a simple tree structure.

You can use view filters to limit what devices or hosts are displayed. This will reduce onscreen clutter.

The icons representing hosts and storage devices use badges and color to convey status information. Badges are added to base icons to signify that storage is partitioned, assigned exclusively, or assigned to a share group. Icon color indicates host and storage partitioned, assigned exclusively, or assigned to a share group. Icon color indicates host and storage availability.

The Share Groups feature is used to assign storage to cluster configurations.

The best ease-of-use feature is the reduction of manual entries, because that's a tedious task and has the greatest potential for operator error.

5.2.2.2   Storage Assignment

Storage is assigned at the LUN level. SAN Manager LM controls storage assignments on the SAN, and doesn't on security mechanisms implemented by particular SAN components.

As mentioned, storage can be assigned when and where it is needed through the drag-and-drop interface. You can also add and remove storage at any time, because no host reboots are required. Storage is available for immediate use after being assigned.

5.2.2.3   Data Consolidation

If SAN Manager LM is used effectively, no storage will be wasted. The right amount of storage for a database will be assigned, and as the database expands, just the right amount of storage is added.

In theory, wasted storage is freed up, and it becomes available to other applications. The goal is optimal use of storage devices.

5.2.2.4   Administration Costs

SAN Manager LM reduces the cost of administering storage because it's a centralized security management solution. Thousands of storage logical unit numbers (LUNs) and hundreds of hosts can be managed as a single SAN. This allows fewer administrators to manage more storage than ever before.

SAN Manager LM is relatively easy to use and that helps storage administration go faster and with less stress. This should result in a more efficient use of the system administrator's time.

5.2.2.5   Redundancy and Flexibility

The SAN Manager LM software architecture has no single point of failure. The SAN configuration database can be mirrored three ways to ensure a copy will always be available. Each host accesses the database independently, eliminating runtime interdependencies between hosts.

SAN Manager LM is compatible with most RAID, JBOD, and tape storage devices because it doesn't depend on particular brands or models of storage devices to implement LUN security. Both native Fibre Channel storage devices and SCSI storage devices behind bridges can be managed.

5.2.3 SAN Manager Device Management (DM)

The HP SureStore E SAN Manager Device Management (DM) application provides comprehensive, centralized management of the SAN environment.

SAN Manager DM uses a management approach taken from HP's Open-View Network Node Manager, used for managing TCP/IP networks.

SAN Manager DM is a Java application, and is the interface for consolidating other management tools, including legacy and browser-based tools.

5.2.3.1 Ease of Use

The SAN Manager DM interface shows a display of SAN devices. If there's a problem with a device, a click of the mouse on the device's icon launches the appropriate device management application to resolve the problem.

SAN Manager DM is an efficient tool for quickly recognizing and resolving device failure issues.

Operators no longer need to run from device to device to troubleshoot problems, add, delete or change storage configurations, or track data center environment changes.

SAN Manager DM can launch device-specific applications and global applications, such as HP OpenView OmniBack II. More than one application can be associated with each SAN device, allowing you to launch one of a set of applications depending on the task to be accomplished. Launched applications may be either Web or server-based.

5.2.3.2   Integration with Other Solutions and Tools

Java technology enables SAN Manager DM to be highly portable. An extensible, open architecture offers enhanced support for servers and storage devices.

Device management applications are easily integrated by way of command line interfaces. The distributed and dynamic loading capabilities that Java offers lend to tighter integration with the graphical user interface and data repository service.

Together, these capabilities provide an environment in which system integrators and other solution providers can easily develop customized SAN management solutions that specifically address their customers' needs.

5.2.3.3   Auto-Discovery and Mapping of Fibre Channel Devices

SAN Manager DM automatically discovers devices that are part of the SAN topology, including server-based Fibre Channel host bus adapters, interconnecting devices and storage devices.

Devices are mapped in an intuitive graphical format at a central console, providing virtually instant visibility into the SAN. Continual automatic discovery assures that changes in the SAN are immediately identified and mapped.

5.2.3.4   Mapping Nonmanaged Devices

As is often the case with new technology, manageability interface standards have not yet been established for Fibre Channel SAN devices. SAN Manager DM ensures that even unmanaged devices are represented on the network map by allowing these devices to be added manually.

5.2.3.5   Creating Custom Views of the SAN

The automatically generated map of the SAN shows all physical connections between devices. This map can be customized into views with drag-and-drop simplicity, so icons are grouped to more accurately reflect their geographical distribution. Once created, custom views can be saved for future use. SAN Manager DM produces both a hierarchical and a graphical representation of the

SAN. Clicking on a device icon changes the map perspective to show which devices are connected to the selected device.

5.2.3.6   Health Monitoring of Devices/Status Monitoring

SAN Manager DM receives device status information from the individual devices and reports it to a central console. Color-coded icons on the SAN map allow IT operators instant recognition of devices that are experiencing a problem or are down. In addition, SNMP traps are generated and can be passed to other management or monitoring applications for action. For example, an alarm can be configured so that when a specified event occurs, a page is sent to notify a system administrator of the problem.

5.2.3.7   Event Monitoring

SAN Manager DM maintains an ongoing log of device events for historical reference. An event browser, similar to the one in HP OpenView Network Node Manager, enables the user to review the detailed events. Events are grouped by categories. The event browser enables the user to filter the event log based on the event source, event severity, time logged, or other attributes. Entries in the event file can be flagged as "acknowledged" to indicate when action has been undertaken for this event.

5.2.3.8   DM Summary

HP SureStore E SAN Manager DM provides comprehensive, centralized management of the SAN environment. SAN Manager DM is an effective solution for enterprise-wide SAN management.

Centralized Console Management of storage devices, no matter what their type, can be accomplished with a single tool that can be used independently of the storage's host.

- Auto-Discovery of Devices—automatically identifies, adds, and maps new devices so the administrator can better utilize all resources.

- Graphical Device Map—graphical maps provide a quick, clear view of the connection between hosts, devices, and components of the SAN infrastructure.

- Real-Time Device Monitoring.

- Launchable Device Icons—a visible alarm lets the administrator know the status of any device and launch applications in order to make changes on the fly.

- Customized Device Maps—groups icons more accurately to reflect their geographical location so you know where the device resides on the SAN.

- Health Monitoring, Alarm Configuration, Event Monitoring, and Event Logs—lets the administrator know what's going on and what's happened on the SAN.

Backup and Restore

This chapter discusses:

- **Why do backups?**
- **SAN demands on backup**
- **The painful rules of backup**
- **SAN backup media**
- **SAN backup devices**
- **SAN backup topologies**

Backup and restore operations are essential. This chapter describes the techniques for backing up SAN storage.

6.1 Why Do Backups?

Backup is a tedious, costly, and usually thankless task in an Information Technology department. Yet there are few who would risk the company's data (and their own job security) by instituting a policy of not backing up.

Storage Area Networks impose new demands on the backup and restore process, yet they also offer new possibilities that may make backup and restore operations simpler and more efficient than ever before.

This chapter reviews the rationale, principles, and building blocks of backup and restore. It then shows how backup and restore operations fit into the world of the SAN.

6.1.1 What's a Backup?

Backup describes an operation that makes a copy of vital data at an optimal time. The term "backup" also describes the collection of copied data, stored safely in case a restore is needed. Data is copied from "primary" storage, typically disk drives, to "secondary" storage, typically tape.

Tape has been the backup medium of choice for about 40 years, owing to its relatively low cost, relatively high density, physical compactness, and ease of transport to storage facilities. This is still true today, despite several drawbacks: inherent slowness in writing to tape, proneness to tape errors, and the limited "shelf life" of tape.

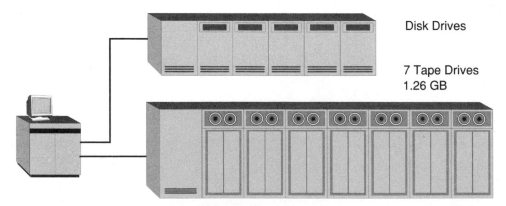

Figure 6-1   The Bad Old Days: Mainframe Backup

In the 1960s, the mainframe operator probably wouldn't have had the luxury of using the shop's complete string of tape drives (Figure 6-1). He or she might have been allocated two or three drives to get all the data from the disks. Hanging tapes to do the backup could take up a significant part of the shift.

Although the equipment is now smaller, the principle hasn't changed. The object is still to copy disk data to tape. The tape drives hold more, but the disk drives can be much larger in capacity (Figure 6-2).

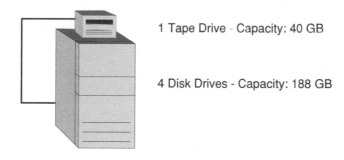

1 Tape Drive - Capacity: 40 GB

4 Disk Drives - Capacity: 188 GB

Figure 6-2 The Bad New Days: Server Backup

In the 1990s and up through today, the system administrator has the same concern: getting all the data on backup media in a relatively short amount of time. Granted, the tape drives are smaller, the tapes are smaller, the tape capacities are higher. However, the disk drives are much larger and there can be many servers (hundreds, potentially thousands) in an enterprise. Forty years since the 1960s and the operator is still changing tapes.

Ideally, the backup is a full backup, a complete snapshot of company data. But full backups take time, and have traditionally required that the system be unavailable to users. As company data grows, full backups take longer and longer to complete. In classic data processing, the company was idle late at night, and therefore full backup was a traditional activity for third-shift computer operators.

Here is a summary of the contemporary "10-tape" method. Your work-group or department may use something quite similar to it. This is taken directly from HP advice to users of DDS (DAT) tape.

There are many systematic methods for regularly backing up data. One of the more common ones is the ten-tape cycle method. It is easy to implement. It also keeps more than one historical copy of the data so that losing one tape does not mean you have lost your data. Assuming a tape life of 100 backup and restore passes per tape, using this method you should have to replace your tapes only once a year.

The method involves maintaining a daily, weekly, and monthly backup. Every three months the monthly tapes are recycled. The advantages of this method are:

- Simplicity. It is very easy to recover data.

- Easy access. Data backed up any time during the past two months can be easily found and restored.

If all the data you wish to back up will fit onto a single tape, you will need ten backup tapes. (Naturally, you will also want extra tapes for archival storage or file transfers.)

If you require more than one tape per backup, you will need ten sets of tapes, with each set composed of the smallest number of tapes that will hold a full backup.

Before making a backup, label each of the ten tapes as follows:

Daily Sets	Weekly Sets	Monthly Sets
Monday	Friday 1	Month 1
Tuesday	Friday 2	Month 2
Wednesday	Friday 3	Month 3
Thursday		

If you need more than one tape to perform a full daily backup, record the tape number (for example, "Tape 1 of 2").

- On Monday, Tuesday, Wednesday, and Thursday, make a full backup to the tape labeled for that day.

- On the first, second, and third Friday of the month, make a full backup to the tape labeled for that day.

- On the fourth Friday of the month, perform the backup on the tape labeled for that month.

- At the end of the fourth month, recycle the monthly tapes. In other words, start again with the tape labeled "Month 1."

For extra security, place each of the Friday and monthly tapes in a fireproof safe, or store them away from the site.

No, that's not a misprint. The above procedure specifies full backups on all cycles. An interesting approach if you don't have a world of data to back up, but do have a world of time to do it in.

An incremental backup copies only what data has changed since yesterday (strictly speaking, since the last backup). This is usually a much smaller amount of data than a full backup, and so requires less time. However, the reduced time needed to back up data may be overtaken by the enterprise's need for more time for active processing. The result is a smaller "backup window."

Incremental backups have spawned a number of complex backup strategies: multiple tape sets, dailies, weeklies, monthlies, etc. With the company's last full backup and a number of incremental backups, company data can be fully restored.

Incremental backups are not superior, in terms of organization and book-keeping, but at least they require less processing time. Here is a six-tape method, requiring only one full backup per week:

Before making a backup, label each of the six tapes as follows:

Daily Sets	**Weekly Sets**
Monday	Friday 1
Tuesday	Friday 2
Wednesday	
Thursday	

If you need more than one tape to perform a daily backup, record the tape number (for example, "Tape 1 of 2").

- Begin by making a full backup of the system on the tape "Friday 1."

- On Monday, Tuesday, Wednesday, and Thursday, make an incremental backup to the tape labeled for that day.

- If you need to restore all data, use the previous Friday's tape, and the incremental tapes made before the data loss. For example, if you need to restore on a Wednesday morning, use the previous Friday's full backup, plus the incremental backups for Monday and Tuesday.

- On Friday, make a full backup of the system on the tape "Friday 2." On each Friday, alternate between "Friday 1" and Friday 2."

- On the fourth Friday of the month, perform the backup on the a Friday tape or on a monthly tape labeled for that month.

- On every Monday, start reusing the daily tapes.

It's difficult to find a data center that doesn't use a combination or variation of the above methods, no matter what the size of the business or the quantity of data involved.

6.1.2 What's a Restore?

Restore describes an operation that copies backed-up data from secondary storage to a primary storage device.

Computing equipment is not perfect, and primary storage can fail. Data can also be lost for other reasons, as described below. So when data is lost, a restore will bring back the last, best copy of company data. A combination of full and incremental backups will restore most, if not all, company data.

Transactions entered between the time of the last incremental backup and the failure of primary storage are lost. So while backup and restore operations are valuable, they are less than perfect. In 24/7 operations, and highly active online transaction processing environments, there remains the possibility of loss of recently entered data.

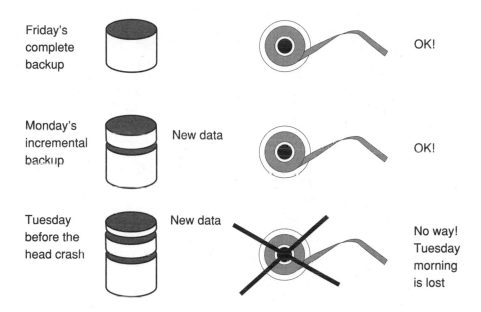

Friday's
complete
backup   OK!

Monday's   New data
incremental   OK!
backup

Tuesday   New data   No way!
before the   Tuesday
head crash   morning
                                          is lost

Figure 6-3   Inability to Restore Today's Data

While the situation in Figure 6-3 is inconvenient, it is usually not disastrous for most sites. However, it poses a severe problem for high-intensity data processing operations. Imagine an online bookstore processing a theoretical one million book orders per hour (OK, 100,000 if you like). Even a loss of ten minutes worth of transactions can be very damaging.

It is no surprise that companies with heavy demands on primary storage use high-availability disk arrays, with redundant power supplies, redundant controllers, redundant fans, embedded RAID technology, and hot spares (disk drives).

Another protection against unrestorable increments is fast disk-to-disk copies (Figure 6-4). Transfers to tape are still done, but secondary disks (also called "target volumes") are used as part of the strategy.

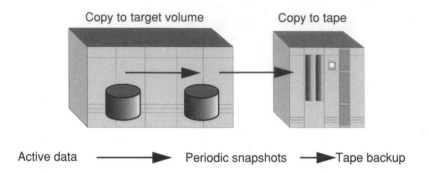

Figure 6-4   Disk-to-disk Copies

The scenario in Figure 6-4 uses a high-end disk array, and it is likely to be seen frequently in SAN configurations. The active data is copied from disk to disk (from source volumes to target volumes), at high speed and with virtually no disruption. Once the snapshot is taken, the target volume can be copied to tape with no disruption to the source volume.

In an ideal world, restores should never take place, and backup data should be quietly archived in a vault, never to be used again. The backup is like a fire extinguisher or a first aid kit. It is valuable in an emergency, but we would hope that that emergency will never happen.

6.1.3 Loss of Data

Now about that emergency. It is not a perfect world, and there is always a risk of loss of data. Experience indicates that the vast majority of losses derive from unexpected failures of media, unexpected failures of hardware, and accidental deletion by human beings. Deliberate destruction of data is far more rare.

In the world of software development, many a programmer has accidentally deleted or overwritten the most recent source code for an important program. Even in the world of desktop applications, critical documents or even a complete small business accounting system can disappear with a careless click of the mouse on the **OK** button.

Modern enterprise servers and mainframes serve a large number of users and have the capacity to hold massive amounts of data in embedded or attached storage. Such quantities and concentrations of data increase the enterprise's exposure to loss of data.

Big enterprises have more people accessing more data more hours per day than small enterprises. The concept of managing gigabytes of data has given way to the concept of terabytes, and petabytes are on the horizon.

Data loss for reasons other than hardware failure is less frequent but certainly can happen. The first is the deliberate destruction of data. It is still relatively easy to deliberately delete an enterprise's critical files. A clever perpetrator can trigger the destruction to happen at a time when he or she is off-site, when business is at a seasonal peak, or both.

The Internet provides new opportunities for data loss, or at least to impede the efficient delivery of data. There are frequent national news reports about people hacking into government and commercial Web sites, usually with the goal of vandalism or disruption of Internet operations. What is not well reported by image-conscious corporations is the theft or destruction of data.

In the old days, it was bad enough to lose the customer master file, containing hundreds of customer records. In modern times, hackers can steal data, destroy data, or deface a site visited by millions of customers daily. This can have consequences ranging from temporary loss of millions of dollars (per hour!) to major embarrassment for a corporation or a government agency. The loss of Web page data can undermine the public's confidence in a company's ability to handle orders, deliver merchandise, and protect customer credit card information.

Lastly, catastrophes (both man-made and natural) can create disastrous data losses. A five-alarm fire will ruin a company's day. A hurricane or earthquake can ruin everyone's day in a whole region.

The economics of such data losses are severe. On a global plane, a company may serve customers around the world, and the quick restoration of data and computer operations is vital to meeting customer needs. On a local plane, employees need their livelihoods in order to rebuild after a disaster, so the company has an obligation to restore operations as quickly as possible, keeping the employees working and reestablishing a normal state of affairs.

6.2 SAN Demands on Backup

Implementation of a SAN can be a real help to an enterprise. However, the more a SAN gives the enterprise in terms of capacity and flexibility, the greater the problem it imposes on backup.

Backing up data from a SAN is like backing up data in conventional storage. However, the SAN typically has a lot more data. Like conventional backup, SAN backup emphasizes completeness, accuracy, speed, and reliability.

6.2.1 Volume of Data

It's nearly impossible to keep up. The volume of data to be backed up is driven by the volume of data stored on disks, and the general rule is that if it can be stored, it will be stored. The best example is the data warehouse, a database essentially dedicated to storing all the company information it can.

Increases in disk capacity occur at every level in the enterprise and you should expect that you'll be called on someday to back it all up.

A 20 GB disk drive is not uncommon on PCs, and there's no reason to believe capacity points in PC disk drives will remain static at a "mere" 20 GB. A business may have thousands of PCs in desktop and laptop form, and if the enterprise has users working at home, the number rises. So if your IT department offers users connected PC backup, then even the PCs alone could pose a terabyte burden on the backup strategy.

Enterprise servers contain multiple, high-capacity disk drives, and whether or not you implement a SAN, embedded storage in the servers will still exist and the servers will still need to be backed up. Like PC disk drives, capacity will continue to be a selling point for server disk drives, and if there is capacity, users will fill it.

This is evident already in mail servers. Most users seem to collect e-mail faster than they can remove it from their in-boxes. Some users think they should save every e-mail message. And it seems that no matter how often you increase mail server storage capacity, the disks fill up again.

The Storage Area Network is scalable without limit. Whether you have a large number of JBODs or a small number of very large disk arrays attached to your SAN, it remains that you are offering your users tremendous capacity for growth, and the users will take you up on the offer.

At this point, Hewlett-Packard's largest mass storage device, the HP Sure-Store E XP256, can contain up to 256 disk drives with up to 1024 LUNs. The capacity points for this device have increased several times since the product was announced. They are changing so fast that the user documentation cannot keep up with them. At the time of this writing, you can populate an XP256 with 47GB drives, yielding about 12 TB of storage.

There's no theoretical limit to how many XP256's you can add to the SAN. Further, there are sure to be larger XP offerings in the future.

There's a big challenge in creating a backup strategy in an environment of rapidly increasing storage. Those who have lived in urban centers know that adding a new lane to a freeway never keeps pace with increased traffic. By the time the new lane opens, there's already too much traffic. And the new lane encourages more people to use that freeway. The same is true with a SAN, so this should be kept in mind when planning for SAN backup and restore.

6.2.2 Zero Downtime: The Need for Speed

Everyone despairs of the time required for backup—users, IT personnel, and management. Therefore, reducing the time required for backup is essential.

The goal is zero downtime backup, a backup that takes place without interrupting processing. This can happen on a SAN with devices and software that permit disk-to-disk copies. Backup takes relatively less time, so more frequent and up-to-date "snapshots" of company data are possible.

Another concern about backup speed is its effect on the speed of other processing. Backup methods that move data from servers and attached storage to the tape library over the LAN slow down LAN performance for users. Therefore a LAN-less backup is desired. Backups burden servers. It would be ideal to minimize that burden, and this can happen on a SAN, using "serverless" backup.

The perception that "tape runs slow" is born out by performance statistics for even the most modern tape libraries. A tape can move through the tape transport only so fast. Again, disk-to-disk copies will minimize a tape library's contribution to slowing down backup.

Another perception of speed is that backup is slow and tedious for human operators. And that's true, too, especially in enterprises where the operators must "change out" tape. Fortunately, backup hardware like tape libraries can dramatically reduce human intervention time in the backup equation. Also, complex backups can be managed with less effort, using management software.

6.2.3 Reliability

In addition to increased volume of data to be backed up and decreased time in which to back up, reliability of the backup must stay at current levels—or increase.

Reliability means two things: 1) all the data requested to be backed up will be backed up, and 2) write operations to backup media must occur with a minimum of errors.

The first concern is addressed by "smart" backup software. As the SAN grows, new storage must be worked into the backup strategy. Products like HP's OmniBack II go a long way toward easing the management headaches that come with expanding storage capacity.

The second concern is addressed first by reliable media. An error rate of 1 error in 10^{12} bits is currently acceptable for DLT tapes, commonly used in backup operations.

However, tape write operations in some SAN configurations are not reliable. In particular, when backup hardware (a tape library) is directly attached to a hub, the FC-AL protocol ("streaming LIPs") can inherently damage the backup process. Switch technology eliminates this concern, and also provides a full bandwidth connection.

6.2.4 Heterogeneous Processors

One promise of the Storage Area Network is that various processors (for example HP-UX servers, Windows 2000 servers, Sun Solaris servers) will be able to access storage devices on the SAN.

Of course that doesn't mean they know or understand each other's file systems, and there's no reason to believe any one OS can effectively manage the backups for LUNs used by other OSs. This is one of the challenges facing SAN development.

6.2.5 Heterogeneous Storage

Unless your site is committed to a one-vendor solution, or you have hired an integrator who promised thorough testing of all SAN elements, you will build and expand your SAN with heterogeneous storage devices. The integrator may use storage devices from different manufacturers, but the implied promise is that they all work together as if they were a one-vendor solution.

The promise of the SAN, too, is that all components, including heterogeneous storage devices, will work together. While a site may use disk storage supplied primarily by one vendor, the backup hardware (tape drives or tape library) and software might come from a different vendor. Hewlett-Packard has made an announcement of its commitment to an open SAN architecture, and we would hope every manufacturer of SAN equipment would agree with and commit to the concept.

6.3 The Painful Rules of Backup

All backup and restore operations, including SAN backup and restore operations, are subject to the "Painful Rules of Backup." These rules must have been formulated by a man named Murphy, who recognized that the universe is far from perfect.

- **Rule 1. You will have a loss of data.**

  You don't know where. You don't know when. However, it *will* happen. You will lose important data. Either file corruption, accidental overwriting, accidental deletion, deliberate deletion, device failure, or volcanic eruption will make some data unavailable.

  There's a great data processing cartoon from the 1970s showing a distraught programmer being consoled by two others. The caption went something to the effect: "Well, you can recode it from the printout." You may personally know that gut-wrenching feeling when a vital file isn't there anymore. It's no great fun to redo source code, reenter the customer database manually, or process customer orders by hand for a few days.

  Obviously, you hope to never find yourself in this position, whether you are dealing with a single source code file, gigabytes of stored video, or 100 TB of business data.

- **Rule 2. Do it. Do it right. Do it right now.**

  You must assure yourself that you have a suitable backup strategy in place and that it's operating successfully right now. This is true whether you have a SAN in place or not. In fact a good pre-SAN backup strategy makes it a bit easier to design for SAN backups.

  Remember, disaster strikes only when you are unprepared, and ironically, if you're prepared, it's not so much of a disaster.

  In the late 1970s, University Computing was promoting its backup package for mainframes. UCC had posters showing a hobo roasting weenies under a railroad bridge. The caption was something like: "What ever happened to Bill after that little problem with the payroll master file?" You don't want to end up like Bill.

Given the sheer volume of data most enterprises have, and given the demand for high speed and reliability, backup and restore is a daunting task. It requires a well-planned backup strategy. As you move to a SAN configuration, this requirement increases.

- **Rule 3. Plan your SAN with backup in mind.**

  Understand the potential for rapid growth of primary storage on a SAN, and plan tomorrow's backup strategy now. Unfortunately, the cards are stacked against you.

  The developers of massive primary storage are outpacing the developers of secondary storage. Increases in disk storage capacity are commonplace; increases in tape capacity are not. In fact, substantial increases in tape capacity are usually considered a generational change.

  The developers of Fibre Channel connectivity are outpacing the developers of secondary storage. And as the current 1 Gbps Fibre Channel evolves to 2 Gbps (which has just been announced for this year) and 4 Gbps, it will be more convenient to store and retrieve more data, and the increased bandwidth will allow more people to do so.

  At the same time, the tape backup process will retain its limitations. The limitations are the relatively slow speed of tapes through the tape drive's transport, and the relatively slow speed of robotic tape changers. The good news is that tape density, compression, and lengths are improving all the time.

- **Rule 4. If you back up, nothing will go wrong. If you don't back up, everything will go wrong.**

  How can this make sense? There is no hard science behind this statement, but many system administrators will support this. Through some sort of information processing magic, the more you back up, the less likely you are to have a data loss.

Or to put it the opposite way, if you don't back something up, there's sure to be a need to restore it. The scope of the problem can range from the unavailability of a 30 KB printer driver to a 10 MB employee database, but it doesn't matter. This seems to be an immutable law of the universe.

Was prevention of data loss easier in the past? Not particularly. Even in the days of punch cards, the unit records (the cards) could be folded, spindled, and mutilated. An operator could drop a tray of cards, usually with a number of them falling in the cracks between the disk drives.

The funniest (if it hadn't been so tragic) case of data loss I (Barry) remember was in the 1970s on Spring Street, the heart of Los Angeles' financial district. During a morning "tickertape" parade, bank employees threw tens of thousands of punch cards out of the office windows. That afternoon, the same bank employees were all on their hands and knees on Spring Street, trying desperately to gather the cards they had thrown out in error!

6.4 SAN Backup Media

6.4.1 Past Backup Media

If we ignore that period of time when punch cards and paper tape were used as backup media, tape has always been the medium of choice for backup. It is dense and relatively inexpensive.

As described in Chapter 2, tape emerged in the 1950s and 1960s as a 9-track, 1200' (or shorter!) open reel medium on 10' (or smaller!) reels. It had a density of 800 bits per inch. The length expanded to 2400' and density increased to 6250 BPI. Through the 1970s, open-reel tape was the only serious medium for backup, and indeed the residence of many batch-processed master files and transaction files.

The operator at an IBM mainframe shop would be known as either the "console commander" or the "I/O hanger," depending on seniority and job responsibilities. The I/O hanger spent the shift "hanging" open-reel tapes on floor-standing tape drives with vacuum columns.

This image of an open-reel tape mounted in a floor-standing tape drive still pervades the public's perception of computing. It's seen in movies and television programs. The spinning reel of tape still says "computer" to most people.

Through the 1980s, there were still plenty of open-reel tape implementations. However, the tape transport mechanism grew smaller, until it took on the shape of a small console (about the size of a toaster oven) or PC-sized unit, which could fit on a desktop.

Over the years, open reel tape gave way to more compact form factors. This includes cassettes, data cartridges (like the little DC-100A), Quarter Inch Cartridge (QIC), 7mm Exabyte and 4mm DAT variations (DDS-1, DDS-2, DDS-3, and DDS-4). At one point, VHS tape was sold as a backup medium.

In all cases, thankfully, there was a move to place the tape in a small, easy-to-handle cartridge. In all cases, the physical size of the tape decreased. These changes made the autoloading, magazine fed tape drive (the grandfather of the tape library) possible.

The introduction of autoloaders raised capacity by using multiple cartridges, and also moved us in the direction of unattended backup.

DDS is still widely used today, and has undergone several generational changes. It's an appropriate medium for smaller operations, in either single-mech or autoloader devices.

In all cases, the recording capacity of the tape increased, due to these technology changes:

- Change from linear to helical scan
- Increase in tape length
- Improved compression algorithms

Speed has increased, due to the introduction of streaming, instead of the stop/start approach to reading and writing tapes.

Look at the evolution of DAT (DDS) tape. The generations are shown in Table 6-1 and compared to open real eight-track tape.

Table 6-1   Evolution of DDS Tape Capacities

Type	Length	Capacity
Open reel	2400 ft	180 MB
DDS-1	90 m	4 GB (2:1 compression)
DDS-2	120 m	8 GB (2:1 compression)
DDS-3	125 m	24 GB (2:1 compression)
DDS-4	125 m	40 GB (2:1 compression)

Each change produced increases in density, capacity, speed, and reliability. However, past media cannot meet backup demands of today's SANs. It takes a combination of DLT and libraries to hold large quantities of them for backup to match the scale of the data to be backed up.

6.4.2 Current Media

DAT (DDS) tape and Digital Linear Tape (DLT) are the media most commonly in use for backup.

DDS tapes are found widely where capacity requirements are relatively small. In many small businesses and corporate workgroups, a single tape drive and a collection of DDS tapes will meet all backup demands.

For example, an HP DAT 40i with a capacity of 40 GB will be found in an HP SureStore E 4000, a network attached storage disk device. That device holds a maximum of six disk drives with a maximum of 18.7 GB/drive. A full backup can be accomplished with three or fewer tapes and manual intervention.

Digital Linear Tape is a high-capacity tape technology that combines large capacity with fairly fast write times. It will be found in configurations ranging from a single mechanism to 700-slot tape libraries with up to 20 tape drives.

HP's DLTtape III cartridge had a capacity of 15 GB native uncompressed, while HP's DLTtape IV cartridge had a capacity of 20 GB uncompressed. Tape libraries that use 20 GB tapes will accept 15 GB tapes for compatibility purposes, but the new, larger tapes are recommended.

HP's current DLTtape for the new tape libraries advertises an 80 GB cartridge capacity. That is, the capacity is 40 GB native and 80 GB compressed, assuming a 2:1 compression ratio.

Product announcements almost always cite maximum capacity, with the assumption that compression will be used. So, we should think of the newest DLT cartridge as an 80 MB cartridge. The caution is that the compression ratio varies with your data and your actual results could vary from the advertising.

Given that HP advertises DLT performance of up to 1,000,000 read/write passes and a guaranteed archival life of 30 years, DLT is the best archival backup medium to date. The price of $89.99 per tape is not daunting—until you start buying thousands of tapes. And doing backups with the highest capacity tape libraries can consume a lot of tapes.

When high-capacity cartridges are deployed in tape libraries, overall storage capacity becomes impressive. In terms of capacity, there are tape libraries that can match the needs of most SANs.

6.4.3 Future Media—Magnetic

A generational change in tape media is now taking place. LTO (Linear Tape-Open) will change the world of the tape medium dramatically and is likely to endure for at least ten years.

Developed jointly by HP, IBM, and Seagate, LTO is an open format tape technology with two design paradigms. The Accelis format is designed for fast access, while the Ultrium format is designed for high capacity (Figure 6-5).

While both formats are valuable, the Accelis format trades reduced capacity for increased speed, which makes it somewhat less interesting for backup; unless speed of retrieval from tape is a critical factor in the operation.

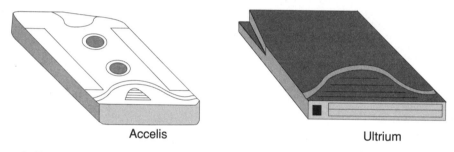

Accelis   Ultrium

Figure 6-5   Accelis and Ultrium Tapes

These tapes have some very interesting capabilities.

6.4.3.1   Ultrium Features

These are the features of the Ultrium LTO format, based on information from the LTO organization's Web page:

- **Form factor.** Approximate cartridge dimensions: 4.1 in x 4.0 in x 0.8 in (105 mm x 102 mm x 21 mm). This makes it smaller than most existing single-reel tape cartridges.

  The single-hub design, it is claimed, allows the cartridge to be "optimally packed with media." By this, we assume it holds a lot of tape.

- **Compression.** LTO technology has a data compression algorithm with two control modes, advertised to maximize compression efficiency.

- **Capacity.** Up to 200 GB capacity (assuming 2:1 compression). The first generation has four cartridge capacities: 20, 60, 100, and 200 GB.

- **Transfer rate.** Ultrium provides for data transfer rates of 20 to 40 MBps for the first generation of the 8-channel version.

- **Cartridge memory** (LTO-CM). The tape has an embedded electronics and interface module that can store and retrieve a cartridge's historical usage and other information. That information is contained in 4 KB of nonvolatile memory. Cartridge memory can store calibration information, manufacturers' data, information about initialization, a redundant file log, and user-defined information.

    You can also get an external reader to retrieve this information without having to insert the cartridge into a drive.

6.4.3.2 Ultrium Internals

The tape has 384 data tracks, divided into four regions (data bands containing up to 96 tracks). Each data band is bounded on top and bottom by a band of servo information.

The servo bands are prewritten on the tape during the manufacturing process. If one servo element becomes defective, or if a portion of the servo code on the tape becomes corrupt, the head will continue to track as a result of the second servo system.

The tape has two levels of error correction that can provide recovery from longitudinal scratches. Also, the Read-While-Write (RWW) capability allows real-time verification of written data.

6.4.3.3 Ultrium Migration Path

Table 6-2 is the declared four-generation roadmap for LTO Ultrium tapes. Hewlett-Packard, IBM, and Seagate point out that they reserve the right to change the information in this migration path without notice.

Table 6-2   Four-Generation Roadmap for Ultrium Tapes

	Generation 1	**Generation 2**	**Generation 3**	**Generation 4**
Capacity (2:1 compression)	200 GB	400 GB	600 GB	1.6 TB
Transfer Rate (2:1 compression)	20 to 40 MBps	40 to 80 MBps	80 to 160 MBps	160 to 320 MBps
Recording Method	RLL 1, 7	PRML	PRML	PRML
Medium	MP	MP	MP	Thin Film

Remember that specifications are subject to change, but certainly the fourth generation of the Ultrium format shows startling capacity and transfer speed, by any of today's standards. If Ultrium's Generation 4 becomes a reality, SAN backups will be much easier to accomplish.

6.4.3.4   Accelis Features

The Accelis format is the fast-access, dual-reel implementation of LTO technology. It has these features:

- **Form factor.** The Accelis tape path is fully contained in the cartridge (it's a dual-reel cartridge), so tape can be loaded at the midpoint instead of the beginning. As a result, there is none of the thread time required for a single-reel cartridge.

- **Fast searches.** Search times are reduced to "sub-10-second averages" because of the dual-reel construction and midpoint loading.

- **Capacity.** An Accelis cartridge has a capacity of up to 50 GB (assuming 2:1 compression).

- **Transfer rate.** Like the Ultrium format, Accelis cites 20 to 40 MB per second (assuming 2:1 compression) for the first generation 8-channel version.

- **Cartridge memory** (LTO-CM).

- **Roadmap.** Like the Ultrium format, the Accelis format is designed with a four-generation road map that provides for up to 400 GB per cartridge (assuming 2:1 compression) in the fourth generation with average time to file under 6.5 seconds.

The LTO organization believes that the Accelis format can handle a wide range of online data inquiry and retrieval applications. However, few think of tape cartridges when thinking of online retrieval. It will be interesting to see if fast access to tape is a concept that resonates with those buying tape equipment.

The LTO group also cites the value of the Accelis format in digital library, data mining, image retrieval, and other read-intensive "near-line" applications. Again, it would be a surprise to see tape, even fast-access tape, become the fashion in data retrieval.

6.4.4 Future Backup Media—Optical

While magneto-optical (MO) storage technology has been with us for a while, and while it's excellent for some applications, it's unlikely to have a serious future in the backup and restore business.

This is because of two factors: first, the mission of tape is clearly backup, occasional restores, and archiving. It does not attempt the tricks advertised for MO. Second, tape is vastly more cost effective.

MO technology will have a place on the SAN, but, in our opinion, it will not be for backup and restore. One manufacturer (HP) states, "For immense amounts of reference data that is viewed only occasionally, magneto-optical storage is the premier choice." True, MO sounds like a good medium for read-only reference data.

MO is useful for online archives, although that sounds like a contradiction in terms. The operative term in optical should not be "archive," but rather "reference data." If you have reference data that needs to be online, obtaining it from tape would be very tedious. Maintaining it on magnetic disk might consume too much space.

The amount of data stored on MO media devices is large, but not colossal. HP's 1200ex optical jukebox, the largest it offers, holds up to 238 5.2 GB optical cartridges, and that's only about 1.2 TB. In all fairness, that jukebox could probably store the service manuals for every type of automobile sold in the world from the invention of the automobile to the present.

Optical is a secure, immediately accessible, permanent storage medium. It is an alternative to paper or fiche, and makes great sense for insurance company source documents, fingerprint archives, and voter signatures. So for library requirements of all kinds, MO provides fairly dense, fairly fast access.

The price of the medium is a little high for backup purposes. HP lists its 5.2 GB Rewritable Optical Disk at $84.99, about the same price as an 80 GB DLT cartridge.

HP has optical libraries with capacities from 16 to 238 cartridges, and they can be integrated in a SAN. Useful, but, in our opinion, not for backup.

6.5 SAN Backup Devices

6.5.1 Tape Libraries

The device of choice for SAN backup and restore is the tape library. A tape library is a "tape hotel" that holds multiple tape cartridges and one or more drive mechanisms. Under robotic control, tapes are moved from storage slots to drives for reading and writing.

The drives in the library are typically DLT4000s, DLT7000s, DLT8000s, or HP9840s. This variety in drive types allows for tradeoffs between capacity and speed. You can have one or the other, but not both, in a drive. However, you can mix drive types in some tape libraries.

When you see tape libraries with paired numbers (such as HP's SureStore E 2/20 or 10/180 models), the first number refers to the maximum number of drives in the unit. The second number refers to the maximum number of cartridges the unit can hold.

At the low end, there are libraries that rackmount in only 5 rack units (U) of space or fit on a desktop. One such model (not made by HP) has one mechanism and 22 DLT cartridges, producing a capacity of 1.76 TB. The manufacturer says the library "gives you the capacity you need for a full month of hands-off backup," which is odd advertising, since there's no way the manufacturer could guess at your monthly backup requirements.

Hewlett-Packard makes tape libraries for midrange and high-end environments. HP midrange tape libraries include:

- HP SureStore E Tape Library 2/20
- HP SureStore E Tape Library 3/30
- HP SureStore E Tape Library 4/40
- HP SureStore E Tape Library 6/60
- HP SureStore E Tape Library 6/100
- HP SureStore E Tape Library 10/180
- HP SureStore E Tape Library 10/588
- HP SureStore E Tape Library 20/700

Models 2/20, 4/40, and 6/60 are newer, based on the same architecture, and can scale from one drive (in the 2/20) to six drives with 20 to 60 cartridge slots. That produces a range of 1.6 TB to 4.8 TB, assuming 2:1 data compression.

Approaching the high end of the midrange is the SureStore E Tape Library 10/180, a newer HP offering that could work well on a SAN. It comes with up to ten DLT8000 drives or six HP9840 drives, and has a maximum capacity of 14.4 TB. It will probably be offered with LTO in the future.

For those who believe there is no substitute for immense capacity, the high-end HP tape library is the 20/700. It has a capacity of about 56 TB, assuming 2:1 compression.

This tape library has some of the high-availability features previously discussed for disk arrays: dual fans, hot-swappable tape drives, hot-swappable power supplies, and dual pathing. That makes it a very suitable candidate for a SAN.

What's the difference between a 20/700 with DLT8000 drives and HP9840 drives? Capacity versus speed.

Table 6-3   DLT8000 vs. HP9840 Drives

	DLT8000	**HP9840**
Number of drives	20	12
Cartridge capacity	40 GB	20 GB
Library capacity	28 TB (native 56 TB (compressed)	14 TB (native) 28 TB (compressed)
Throughput	216 GB/hr (native 432 GB/hr (compressed)	360 GB/hr (native) 720 GB/hr (compressed)

This scale of tape library would be a good match for backing up data from a high-end disk array, such as HP's XP256 (Figure 6-6).

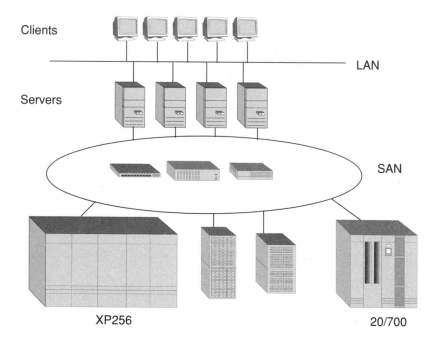

Figure 6-6   20/700 and XP256 in a SAN

6.6 SAN Backup Topologies

It is fairly simple to integrate tape libraries into the SAN, although there are certain connectivity limitations. However, tape library technology is changing every day, so these limitations may soon disappear.

6.6.1 Connectivity Limitations

Almost all tape libraries are SCSI devices. Integrating them into a SAN requires FC/SCSI bridges. The topology examples in this section show bridges in use.

HP's largest tape library is no exception. The descriptive material for the SureStore E Tape Library 20/700 says the device is "part of the HP Equation architecture, *integrating with SureSpan Fibre Channel bridges* [italics added] and hubs for flexible configurations, speed, and distance, with SureDesign Storage Node Manager for proactive diagnostics and centralized management."

However, things are changing. As this book goes to press, manufacturers are starting to announce native Fibre Channel tape libraries for SANs.

6.6.2 Hub Limitations

Tape libraries do not do well on a Fibre Channel Arbitrated Loop (FC-AL). Connecting the tape library to a switch is a far better choice.

Why? The first concern is bandwidth. Fibre Channel Arbitrated Loop allows up to 126 node ports to be connected to the loop. There is a single connection between a pair of ports at any point in time. Since the loop's bandwidth is shared by all participating ports on the loop, any individual port will be able to realize only a portion of the rated bandwidth. For the time the two ports "own" the loop, they get all the bandwidth, but they don't own the loop all the time.

This differs from a Fibre Channel switched-fabric topology, in that ports on the fabric take full bandwidth without sharing. A fabric switch currently costs about four times as much as a hub (about 2.5 to 3 times as much per port).

The second concern is the potential for interrupting the backup operation. In a Fibre Channel Arbitrated Loop, a tape backup in progress can be interrupted by the dynamics of the FC-AL (for example, a LIP occurs when a server is power cycled).

Error handling in the backup application needs close attention to ensure that data loss doesn't occur and that a failed command is recoverable. To prevent a backup or restore operation failure, the backup application software must be able to recover from such a change on the loop.

FC-AL activities, such as power-cycling servers, hot-plugging devices, error states, and other changes can be factors that can cause the system to rearbitrate or cause a LIP to occur. This might interfere with the data transfer to a tape.

A LIP can cause a SCSI command to fail, thereby causing a backup failure. The application informs the operator that the tape operation has failed. To avoid the chance of a tape backup failure, the system administrator must select applications that can handle error recovery and a system environment with stable conditions.

To avoid all this, try one of the following:

- Connect the tape library directly to a server

- Connect the tape library directly to a server using a bridge

- Connect the tape library to a hub of its own

- Connect the tape library to a fabric switch

6.6.3 Straightforward Backups

Let's begin with a Fibre Channel version of a traditional attached-device SCSI configuration (Figure 6-7).

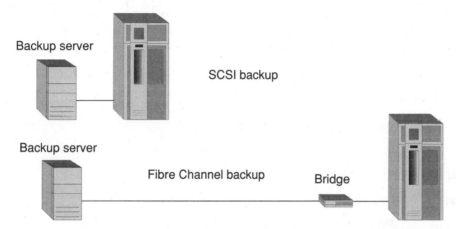

Using an FC4/2 bridge allows a Fibre Channel connection and longer distances

Figure 6-7   Fibre Channel Server Backup

There is an advantage in distance between devices, providing a distance of up to 500 meters between the server and the bridge, plus another 25 meters of SCSI cable at the tape library end. This permits you to locate the tape library in a separate room or on a separate floor.

Backup of other servers takes place by passing data through the backup server over the LAN.

What do we mean by "over the LAN?"

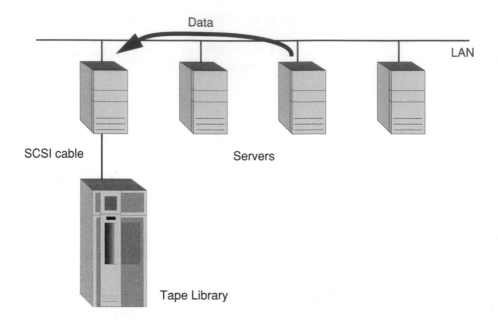

Figure 6-8   Backup Over the LAN

When traditional backup is done over the LAN (Figure 6-8), data on embedded disks and directly-attached storage makes its way to the tape library over the LAN connection. Throughput is slower for the backup, and network bandwidth is consumed. Clients who were already feeling performance bottle-necks will feel them more intensely.

6.6.4   Device Sharing

The backup possibilities are more flexible with Fibre Channel and a bridge (Figure 6-9). The FC4/2 bridge makes it easy for two servers to share a tape library.

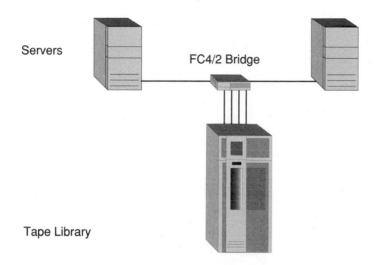

Figure 6-9   Two Servers Share One Tape Library

Both servers can be backed up without requiring data to move across the LAN. Other servers in the configuration would still be backed up over the LAN.

However, if we use two FC 4/2 bridges, we can allow four servers to share a tape library (Figure 6-10).

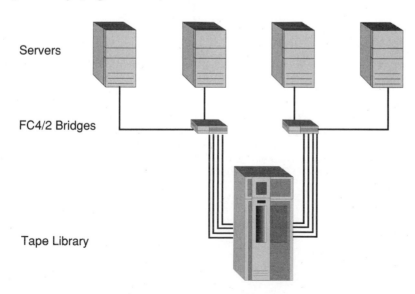

Figure 6-10   Four Servers Share a Tape Library

6.6.5 Backing Up the SAN

But where, you might ask, has the SAN gone? It's still there, as the following illustration shows.

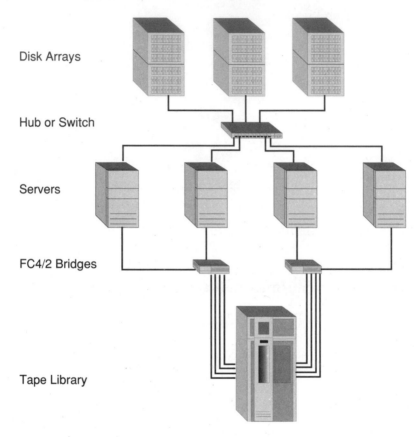

Figure 6-11   Backup Topology with a SAN

In this configuration (Figure 6-11) all servers share all disk devices. They also all access a tape library. It's a high performance backup solution, and backup traffic is eliminated from the LAN.

6.6.6 Vaulting

Your site may require vaulting of secondary storage devices and media in a different room or building than the servers. Here is a distance solution that requires only switches and bridges.

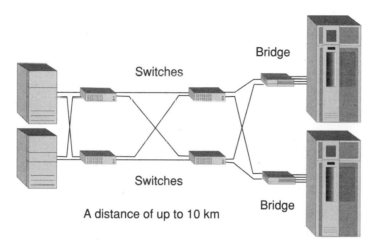

Figure 6-12   Two Servers and Two Tape Libraries

(The SAN storage devices are not illustrated.)

In Figure 6-12, the distance attainable is 10 km over a Fibre Channel connection, using switches. It's a switched, full-bandwidth solution. It provides for double pathing and two libraries in the vault.

Backup of the two servers shown and SAN storage takes places directly. Backup of embedded storage in other servers still takes place over the LAN.

6.6.7 Zero Downtime Backup

A high-end disk array, such as the XP256, has capabilities that can improve the backup process by shortening backup time and making it possible for more frequent "snapshots" of the data to be taken.

Zero Downtime Backup (sometimes called Zero Impact Backup) requires installation of the HP Business Copy XP software on the system and HP's OmniBack II software.

Zero Downtime Backup would be an ideal scenario for SAP R/3 and Oracle databases. The users can continue to access their data during backup. In addition, we would hope for minimum performance degradation for the Oracle and SAP R/3 databases.

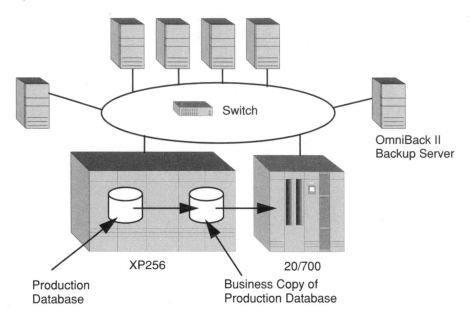

Figure 6-13   Zero Downtime Backup

The solution shown in Figure 6-13 provides a comprehensive split-mirror backup to separate the production environment from the backup and recovery environment. Business Copy XP creates mirror images of active production volumes. Then OmniBack II performs a backup on the business copy, while the database applications continue to run with no performance degradation.

A zero impact backup includes the following five steps:

1.   The database is put into backup mode. This guarantees a consistent version of the data on the business copy.

2.   OmniBack II initiates a split of the ongoing mirroring of data between the source and the target volumes.

3.   After a successful split, the database can be taken out of backup mode.

While the database is in backup mode, the application can still access the data, but performance is slightly decreased during this process. Usually, the database is in backup mode for about five to ten minutes.

4. Now the OmniBack II backup server can perform the backup from the business copy. This process is totally independent from the application host.

5. When the backup is finished the mirror can be resumed and the business copy of the data is resynchronized with the database.

6.6.8 Disaster Recovery

For full disaster recovery, HP SureStore E Continuous Access XP software mirrors data transactions from a primary XP256 to a target XP256, typically in a separate location (Figure 6-14).

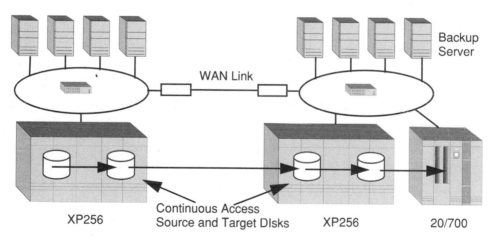

Figure 6-14   Disaster Recovery with Continuous Access XP

The target XP256 may also run SureStore E Business Copy XP software, so the remote site will perform the backup from the business copy.

The OmniBack II backup software allows the backup to be conducted on the remote XP256 disk array at the disaster recovery site. Both the active business application at the local site and the backup process at the remote site retain maximum throughput and full performance. The backup server is attached to the target XP256.

CHAPTER 7

Industry Implementations

This chapter discusses:

- **So now we have one; what do we do with it?**

- **General SAN implementations**

- **Special SAN implementations**

The SAN is not a theoretical construct; it exists in many business sectors and can dramatically increase efficiency. Some SAN-based data management techniques, such as backup or disaster recovery, cross major industry sectors.

7.1 So Now We Have One; What Do We Do with It?

Isn't that the way it always is? Some new technology is developed that can potentially help your enterprise, and all of a sudden there are a myriad of questions that need to be answered.

- How can this new technology help my business?
- How can it be deployed in our environment?
- What software applications take advantage of this new technology?

These are just a few of the questions that are being asked about SANs right now. We probably won't answer all of these to your satisfaction here; however, by discussing a few known industry implementations it may help you focus on implementation in your environment.

Anytime these types of questions are asked, the answer invariably is, "It depends." I say this because the first step in answering these questions is to know the variables in your own environment and where you are going in the future. Therefore your first two questions should be:

- Where's our enterprise now?
- What's our road map to the future?

Once you have answered these questions for your own operation or industry, then you can answer the questions regarding the new technology.

Now, having said all that, let's take a look at some of the ways Storage Area Networks can and are being used.

The SAN capabilities to be exploited are:

- Speed—How fast do you need to access your data?
- Distance—How far apart do your storage devices need to be from your computer systems?
- Continuous availability—Do your databases and applications need to be online 24/7?

- Sharing—Do different servers need to share data or devices?

7.1.1 Speed

We have discussed in previous chapters the I/O transfer protocols, such as SCSI. We have explained that Fibre Channel is much faster in transferring I/O than these other protocols. Therefore, if accessing data really fast is a requirement in your environment, then a Fibre Channel SAN is your answer.

Remember, Fibre Channel currently runs at 1 Gbps; the ANSI standard for Fibre Channel defines a theoretical speed of up to 4 Gbps. So Fibre Channel is fast, and will get faster. Of course, speeds will depend greatly on the design of the components connected within the topology and the specific function for which they are connected.

7.1.2 Distance

If extending the distance between devices is an issue in your environment, then a Fibre Channel SAN can possibly be your answer. Cascaded hubs and switches can increase distances between the servers and the devices being used in the SAN.

For example, if you have a server in one building and the database for that server resides on a storage device in another building, then a SAN may be the right answer for this application. Even if the storage device is a SCSI device, it can still be part of the SAN by using a SCSI bridge to connect it to the SAN.

7.1.3 Availability

Continuous availability or high availability is vital for some applications. E-business and automated teller machines don't shut down at 5:00 P.M., so there's no such thing as doing hardware maintenance on the night shift. High availability storage subsystems use redundant components and RAID hardware or software. These devices can be rather expensive, but in some environments they are absolutely necessary because data must always be accessible.

High availability requirements continually create a higher demand for SAN functionality, mainly because it's easy to scale the SAN with more and more high availability storage.

7.1.4 Sharing

One of the primary drivers for SAN adoption is the concept of sharing data or devices. Sharing reduces the need to have two or more of any one thing, such as a database or the storage system it runs on.

For example, a company may need to provide its customer database to many different internal divisions and regional sales offices. This requires duplication not only of the database, but distribution of the duplicate data to duplicate hardware at the remote sites. Of course there's a constant need for resynchronization of centralized and distributed data as the customer records change.

Another area of sharing is the hardware—the storage device itself and the server using the device. Some companies purchase their hardware from only one vendor for a given application. For example, they would purchase an NT server and an associated storage device from the same vendor. Then for another application, say in a UNIX environment, they would purchase a UNIX server and associated storage device from another vendor.

In this scenario, you wouldn't want to have to buy different storage devices for different servers. What that amounts to is wasted money, floor space, and so on. Heterogeneous SANs can and do address issues like this.

- *Sharing a tape device*. A tape library is expensive and need not be used exclusively by one server. It usually contains more than one tape drive and many tape cartridge slots. Multiple servers can access the different tape drives at the same time to accomplish their read/write operations.

- *Sharing different disks in the same device*. Using certain disk array configuration tools in conjunction with SAN management tools, the disks within a disk array can be divided for use among different applications or servers.

- *Sharing the same data between servers or applications.* The "Holy Grail" of sharing. This is when two servers have a need to access the same data. Then it's great if they can both read and write to the same LUN.

7.2 General SAN Implementations

There are certain general types of SAN implementations. You are likely to see them in any large IT operation, regardless of the industry sector. The next few pages will discuss several major ones.

7.2.1 NT Consolidation

Consolidating and centralizing server and storage assets through the creation of clusters can satisfy some of the sharing needs. The clustering concept is a key for users who need high server availability.

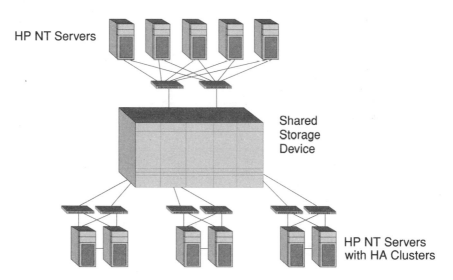

Figure 7-1 NT Consolidation

International Data Corporation defines four principal types of clustering:

- High-availability clustering—system managed failover to another node within the cluster.

- Administrative clustering—management and allocation of resources from across the cluster.

- Application clustering—management of a specific application across a cluster through tight integration of its own automated program interface (API).

- Scalability clustering—a specific workload spread across multiple nodes with the use of system functions.

7.2.2 Mission Critical Application Server

"Mission critical" refers to that data or application that is so absolutely necessary to the survivability of the business that if the data is lost or the application goes down, so does the business.

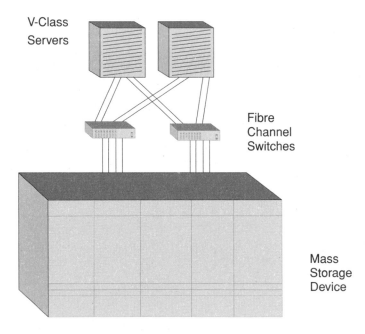

Figure 7-2   Mission Critical Implementation

Therefore, environments supporting mission critical applications need their components and connectivity to be as robust as possible. This implies the implementation of dual pathing (HBAs and cables) and redundancy of infrastructure components (hubs and switches) to ensure the data flow is uninterrupted.

When implementing higher levels of availability to meet business demands, remember that the cost of equipment and associated components increases with the amount of availability needed. However, this may be cost-justified if the downtime costs for your enterprise are high.

7.2.3 High Availability Application Server

"High availability" implies that your data and devices are available for use at all times. It also means there is no single point of failure, either in the components themselves or in the connectivity of the components.

High availability also refers to the ability to allocate or remove resources to and from the SAN, to recover from breakdowns or expand for growth without impacting performance or the accessibility of data. High availability comes built in to the hardware in the form of multiple components within a device (for example, dual power supplies in a disk array).

Sometimes high availability comes in the form of software; for example, an application that runs between two servers in a cluster. The application knows when one server fails and automatically switches control over to the remaining good server.

Another example would be a software package that automatically creates a mirror image of a valuable database from one disk array to another or to another LUN within the same disk array.

7.2.4 Disaster Recovery/Backup

Disaster recovery and data backup are two of the hottest subjects in the industry today. Figure 7-3 demonstrates a possible solution that SANs provide. Here, there is a simple direct connection of servers to a tape library, capable of simultaneously moving data from more than one disk array to the tape library.

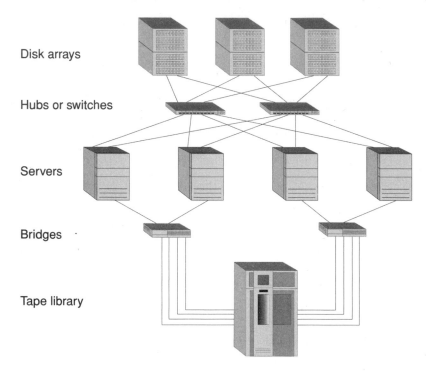

Figure 7-3   Disaster Recovery/Backup

All businesses need to protect their data. It is absolutely critical for data to be backed up in order to be prepared for disaster recovery. Whether the backup is done in the same room, across campus, or at a geographically remote site, it is a necessary evil.

This is a complicated subject, and has been covered in detail in Chapter 6. However, it's illustrated here again, as it is one of the primary driving forces for SANs. Figure 7-3 shows tape library sharing by the servers' Fibre Channel connections (useful for distance) and FC/SCSI bridges (useful for compatibility).

Native Fibre Channel tape libraries, with a direct connection to the SAN, have been announced and are on the immediate horizon.

Zero downtime and instant recovery are the two most frequent discussion topics of disaster recovery. No one wants his or her system to be down for any amount of time; when the system goes down, data must be instantly accessible by another system.

7.3 Special SAN Implementations

There are SAN implementations that appear specialized, because of the severe processing demands of some applications. Those applications need extreme capacity and speed.

The paradox is that most general applications would appreciate a little more in the way of capacity and speed, so today's special SAN implementation has a way of becoming tomorrow's norm. At some point there will be no such thing as a "specialized SAN implementation."

For example, a data warehouse is a storage-intense application, traditionally limited to larger enterprises with the resources to assemble outrageously large collections of data and go exploring. However, with SAN capabilities, medium and smaller enterprises have the potential for making a data warehouse part of their operation.

The same is true with motion picture and video production. Today, it's a specialized application, and a natural place for a SAN. Tomorrow, stored video may be employed widely in nonentertainment applications.

7.3.1 Data Warehousing/Data Mining

A data warehouse is a large collection of enterprise data, managed by a relational database running on a high-performance server. The underlying assumption is that enterprises collect a lot of information, which, if subjected to complex analysis, could help in the decision-making process.

Although the warehouse may be small in size at the start, it's assumed that the company will add a substantial amount of data to it daily. Because the warehouse always grows in size, storage for a data warehouse should be highly scalable. This is a natural application for a SAN, as it's easy to add storage devices. You can increase the number of devices, the capacity of devices, or both.

Data mining tools are used to research data in the data warehouse to find patterns, classifications, and associations. Data mining can help retail businesses see purchase patterns, payment patterns, and the relationships among various purchased items.

Data mining has been quite useful in the retail industry to analyze consumer buying patterns and form marketing programs to take advantage of the analysis results. For instance, data mining can find patterns in your data to answer questions like:

- What item purchased in a given transaction triggers the purchase of additional related items?

- How do purchasing patterns change with store location?

- What items tend to be purchased using credit cards, cash, or check?

- How would the typical customer likely to purchase these items be described?

- Did the same customer purchase related items at another time?

Once the buying patterns have been discovered, the retailer can use this information to tailor a marketing strategy that appeals to each type of buyer, thereby maximizing profits or minimizing costs through optimizing inventory management.

Supermarkets are experimenting with "clubs." When you join the "club," you are issued a barcoded card to be presented when you make purchases. The number is tied to your name, address, e-mail, and other information, and presumably every purchase you make can be linked to you. Store discount coupons arc gone, so the only way you can save on purchases is by presenting your "club" card.

Whether this data collection is useful is up to the supermarket chains. However, it suggests that a lot of data is being collected daily. From that we reason that supermarket chains have big data warehouses, and would suspect that a SAN of ever-increasing capacity is central to the picture.

The retail industry is not the only industry to take advantage of data mining. Other uses for data mining include: risk assessment and portfolio management in the finance industry; fraud detection and policy assessments in health insurance; and optimization, scheduling, and process control in manufacturing.

7.3.2 Video and Motion Picture Production

The most efficient way to edit video and motion pictures is in a digital editing suite. This requires large amounts of storage, and a SAN is the ideal way to accomplish the task.

When footage is digitized and stored on the SAN, multiple editors can work on the same project without breaking it into parts and downloading the video to different workstations.

Transoft Networks of Santa Barbara, CA (recently acquired by Hewlett-Packard), says:

> FibreNet FC can support multiple streams of compressed or uncompressed video from a network with shared storage. This makes it an ideal media environment for a number of non-linear video, audio, animation, and graphics editing applications. FibreNet FC allows multiple artists to work on the same source footage, without being interrupted by sneakernet, searching for shuttles, or duplicating footage. Valuable editing time can be spent on visual creativity instead of media management; footage can be viewed and mastered at ideal resolutions. The combination of speed and ability to collaborate on projects results in clear cost savings and increase in productivity.

What you want in video editing is simultaneous access to the same media files from multiple editing stations. This is superior to the time and effort it takes to place copies of material on multiple local disks. It makes sense that a SAN would be used for video applications.

HP SAN Hardware Products

This chapter discusses:

- **Hewlett-Packard's Fibre Channel chips**
- **Fibre Channel host bus adapters**
- **FC-AL hubs**
- **Disk arrays**
- **XP256 disk array**
- **Tape libraries**
- **FC-SCSI bridges**
- **Fibre Channel switches**

This chapter catalogs the principal SAN products available from Hewlett-Packard and shows how they can be implemented in your SAN.

8.1 Hewlett-Packard's Fibre Channel Chips

8.1.1 Overview

Hewlett-Packard began shipping the Tachyon IC in early 1995; today it is the industry's leading Fibre Channel controller. From this evolved the Tachyon TL IC, a 64-bit PCI-to-Fibre Channel controller that focuses on arbitrated loop topologies for cost-effective, Fibre Channel mass storage designs. Both of these ICs implement the Tachyon family architecture.

8.1.2 Tachyon HPFC-5000C

8.1.2.1 Product Highlights

- Single chip Fibre Channel interface
- Supports both networking and mass storage implementations
- Complete hardware-based design optimized for Fibre Channel
- Released to production June 1996

8.1.2.2 Description

The Tachyon controller IC, HPFC-5000C, supports arbitrated loop, fabric, and point-to-point topologies; Class 1, 2, and 3 services; and quarter, half, and full-speed Fibre Channel data rates. The IC also provides on-chip support of FCP for SCSI initiators and targets and hardware assists for TCP/UDP/IP networking. Performance is optimized within the IC through complete concurrency with eight internal DMA channels and full duplex processing.

First released by HP to customers for development in early 1995, the Tachyon IC is currently designed in by more than 30 OEMs and has become the de facto controller IC choice for Fibre Channel.

Figure 8-1 Hewlett-Packard's Fibre Channel Chips

8.1.3 Tachyon TL Controller HPFC-5100

8.1.3.1 Features

- Second generation controller IC, based on HP's Tachyon architecture
- Targeted to Fibre Channel Arbitrated Loop (FC-AL) designs, including Public Loop support
- Supports Class 2 and 3 services
- 1 Gbps Fibre Channel rate
- Full duplex support with parallel inbound and outbound processing
- 32/64-bit PCI interface, compliant with PCI v2.1
- Complete hardware handling of entire SCSI I/O via FCP on-chip assists
- Full Initiator and Target mode functionality

8.1.3.2   Description

The HPFC-5100, Tachyon TL, is a second-generation controller that leverages HP's experience in Fibre Channel, established with the original Tachyon controller. Tachyon TL focuses on mass storage applications that require FC-AL, Class 3 and 2 (ACK0), and SCSI upper layer protocol handling. Coupled with a high performance 32/64-bit PCI bus interface, Tachyon TL provides a cost-effective, high-performance mass storage solution.

Tachyon TL continues with the Tachyon architecture, a complete hardware-based state machine design. This architecture avoids on-chip microprocessor performance issues of a single processing resource, processor cycles per second, and access times to firmware. Rather, the Tachyon architecture is designed to realize the full potential of Fibre Channel. Tachyon TL provides the highest levels of concurrency by way of numerous independent functional blocks providing parallel processing of data, control, and commands. In addition, these blocks process at hardware speeds versus firmware speeds and automate the entire SCSI I/O in hardware. The result is minimized latency and I/O overhead, coupled with the highest levels of parallelism to provide maximum I/O rates and bandwidth.

8.1.3.3   FC-AL Features

In addition to the high performance architecture, Tachyon TL offers second-generation Fibre Channel features, such as Public Loop, Auto Status, multiple I/Os in the same loop arbitration cycle, loop map, loop broadcast, and loop directed reset. These features allow the designer to achieve higher performance in an arbitrated loop topology.

8.1.3.4 Physical Layer

The physical layer interface is the popular 10-bit wide specification that allows interfacing to a low-cost serializer/deserializer (SerDes) IC. This is the same physical layer interface that is popular on Fibre Channel disk drives today due to its quality gigabit signaling, small form factor, and low cost.

8.1.3.5 Applications

- Motherboard integration
- Host bus adapters
- Storage subsystems
- I2O designs

8.1.4 Tachyon Block Diagrams

Tachyon is a fundamental building block, compatible with Hewlett-Packard's Fibre Channel solution, which includes interface controllers, physical link modules, adapters, switches, and disk drives.

The Tachyon architecture supports both networking and mass storage connections. It is a low-cost, high-performance solution with low host overhead.

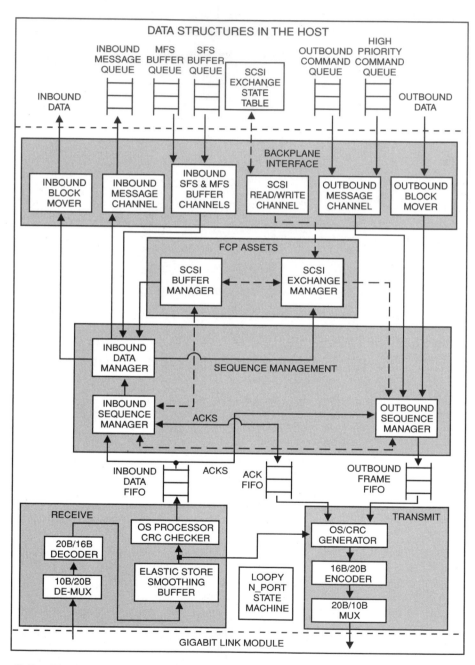

Figure 8-2   Tachyon Internal Block Diagram

8.1.4.1 Features

- Single chip Fibre Channel interface (no I/O processor required)
- Supports 1062.5, 531, and 266 MBaud links
- Supports three topologies: direct connect, fabric, and Fibre Channel Arbitrated Loop (FC-AL)
- Supports Fibre Channel Class 1, 2, and 3 services
- Supports up to 2-Kbyte frame payload for all classes of service
- Sequence segmentation/reassembly in hardware
- Automatic ACK frame generation and processing
- On-chip support of FCP for SCSI Initiators and Targets
- Supports up to 16,384 concurrent SCSI I/O transactions
- Compliant with Interned MIB-II network management
- Direct interface to industry standard 10- and 20-bit Gigabit Link Modules (GLM)
- Hardware assists for TCP/UDP/IP networking
- Parity protection on internal data path
- Eight internal DMA channels
- Full duplex internal architecture that allows Tachyon to process inbound and outbound data simultaneously

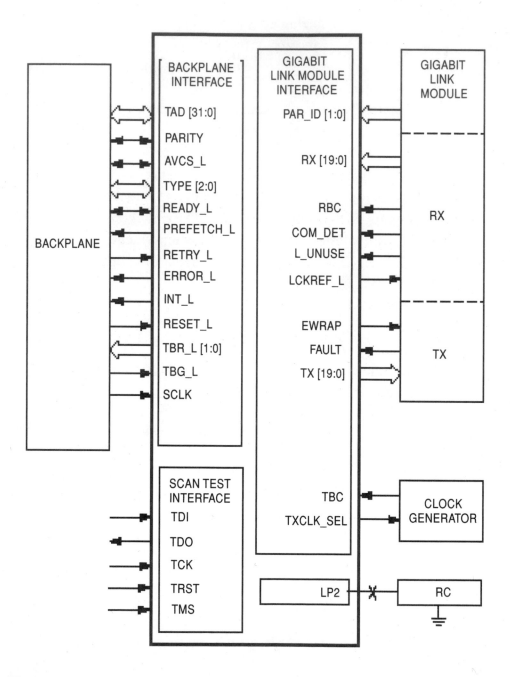

Figure 8-3   Tachyon Pin-out Block Diagram

8.1.4.2 Specifications

- System Clock Frequency:
  - 24 to 40 MHz backplane operation

- Operating Temperature:
  - 0 to 50 degrees C @ 0 m/s airflow
  - 0 to 70 degrees C @ 1.5 m/s airflow

- Testability:
  - Full internal scan path
  - IEEE standard 1149.1 Boundary Scan

- Packaging:
  - 208-pin metal quad flat pack

- Standards:
  - Intended to be compliant with ANSI standards and FCSI/FCA profile definitions

(Hewlett-Packard reserves the right to alter specifications, features, capabilities, functions, and even general availability of the product at any time.)

8.2 Fibre Channel Host Bus Adapters

8.2.1 A3404A Host Bus Adapter

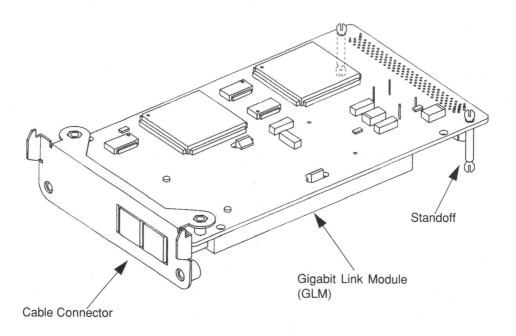

Standoff

Gigabit Link Module
(GLM)

Cable Connector

Figure 8-4   A3404A Fibre Channel Adapter

This Fibre Channel Adapter (FCA) is designed for K-Class systems, models K2xx, K3xx, K4xx, and K5xx. It is a full speed (1063 Mbps), shortwave, non-OFC device. See Table 8-1 for a complete list of supported systems.

Although it is similar to the product used for T-Class systems, this adapter has a different bulkhead and standoffs near the rear connector for shock and vibration protection. It cannot be interchanged with T-Class adapters.

8.2.2   A3636A Host Bus Adapter

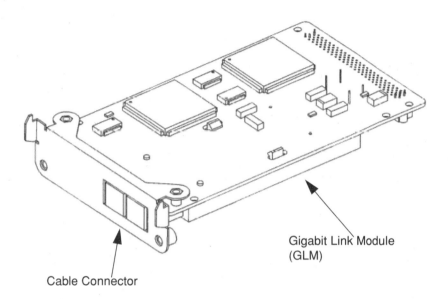

Figure 8-5   A3636A Fibre Channel Adapter

This FCA is designed for T-Class systems, model T600. It is a full-speed (1063 Mbps), shortwave, non-OFC device. See Table 8-1 for a complete list of supported systems.

Although it is similar to the product used for the K-Class systems, this adapter has a different bulkhead and no standoffs near the rear connector. It cannot be interchanged with K-Class adapters.

8.2.3   A3591A Host Bus Adapter

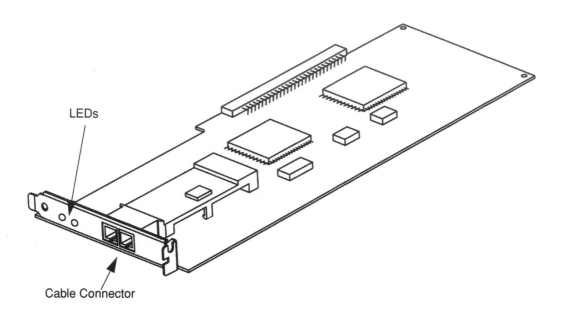

Figure 8-6   A3591A Fibre Channel Adapter

This Fibre Channel Adapter is designed for A-Class and D-Class systems. It is a full-speed (1063 Mbps), shortwave, non-OFC device. See Table 8-1 for a complete list of supported systems.

8.2.4 A3740A Host Bus Adapter

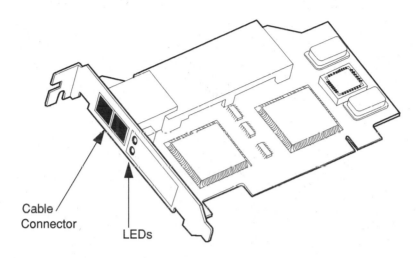

Cable
Connector

LEDs

Figure 8-7   A3740A Fibre Channel Adapter

This Fibre Channel Adapter (FCA) is designed for A-, N-, and V-Class systems. It is a full-speed (1063 Mbps), shortwave, non-OFC device. See Table 8-1 for a complete list of supported systems.

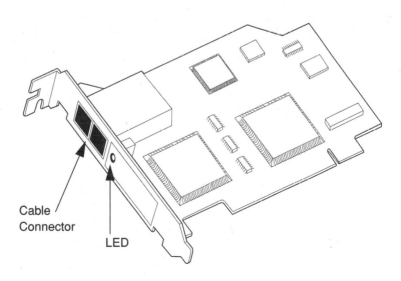

Cable
Connector

LED

Figure 8-8   A3740A Fibre Channel Adapter (New Revision)

8.2.5   A5158A Host Bus Adapter

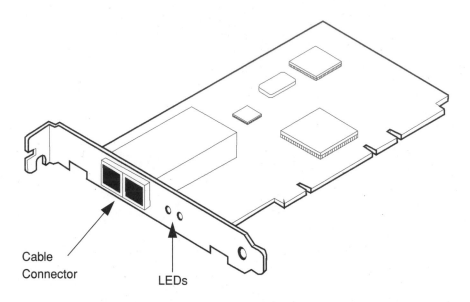

Cable
Connector

LEDs

Figure 8-9   A5158A Fibre Channel Adapter

This Fibre Channel Adapter (FCA) is designed for L-, N-, and V-Class systems. It is a full-speed (1063 Mbps), shortwave, non-OFC device. See Table 8-1 for a complete list of supported systems.

Table 8-1   Supported Systems

	Supported SPUs	**Slot**	**Characteristics**	**Connector**
A3404A	K-class, HP-UX 10.20 or 11.0. Boot support only on HP-UX 11.0.	HSC	1063 Mbps, shortwave, non-OFC	SC Duplex
A3591A/B	A-class, D-class, HP-UX 10.20 or 11.0. No boot support on the A-class. Boot support for D-class on HP-UX 11.0 with A3591B. A3591B support on A-class models (A-180, A-400, A-500) and only on certain D-class models.			
A3636A	T-600 class, HP-UX 10.20 or 11.0.			
A3740A	A-class, N-class, and V-class, HP-UX 11.0.	PCI		
A5158A	L-class, N-class, and V-class, HP-UX 11.0.			

8.3 FC-AL Hubs

Figure 8-10   A3724A/A4839A FC-AL Hub

The FC-AL hub is available in shortwave (S10) and longwave (L10) models. Both models have ten ports, and are available in standalone or factory-racked configurations. The AZ models are the factory-racked models.

8.3.1 Features

- The shortwave hub has ten non-OFC, shortwave optical transceivers.

- The longwave hub has nine non-OFC, shortwave optical transceivers and one non-OFC, longwave optical transceiver.

- Local retime and regeneration of transmit signals to prevent accumulation of jitter and improve the signal.

- Reliable, automatic bypass of failed nodes; dynamic recognition of newly added or removed nodes, with a controller in each port permitting the bypass of a port if the port fails signal validity tests.

- Active loop reconfiguration when a node to an arbitrated loop is added, removed, or moved.

- Plug-and-play capability, allowing the hub to connect to compatible servers and other FC-AL devices while they are operating. FC-AL devices can be added or removed while the hub is active.

8.3.2 S10 Shortwave Hub (HP A3724A/AZ)

The shortwave hub supports 10 non-OFC (non-open fiber control) short-wave FC-AL connections. In arbitrated loop topology, the data rates and wavelength between ports must be the same. The shortwave hub supports only gigabit shortwave to gigabit shortwave connections using fiber cables.

For the shortwave hub, Hewlett-Packard recommends 50 micron multimode fiber cable for new installations, but supports 62.5 micron multimode fiber cable with SC-style connectors in existing installations. Installations can mix 50 micron and 62.5 micron cables.

Using a 50 micron multimode cable, the shortwave hub supports distances up to 500 meters between a server host and the hub, between a hub port and a connected FC-AL device, and between two hubs. The maximum distance between a host server and FC-AL devices connected to cascaded shortwave hubs is 1500 meters.

8.3.3 L10 Longwave Hub (HP A4839A/AZ)

The longwave hub supports nine non-OFC, shortwave devices and a second longwave FC-AL hub. The longwave hub supports shortwave gigabit to short wave gigabit connections from ports 1 through 9 using fiber cables. The longwave hub also supports a longwave hub to longwave hub connection from the longwave port.

For the longwave port, Hewlett-Packard recommends 9 micron single mode fiber cable. For ports 1 through 9, Hewlett-Packard recommends 50 micron multimode fiber cable for new installations but supports 62.5 micron multimode fiber cable with SC-style connectors in existing installations.

For ports 1 through 9, the longwave hub supports distances of up to 500 meters between the port and a connected FC-AL device. For the longwave port, the longwave hub supports distances of up to 10 kilometers between two long-wave hubs.

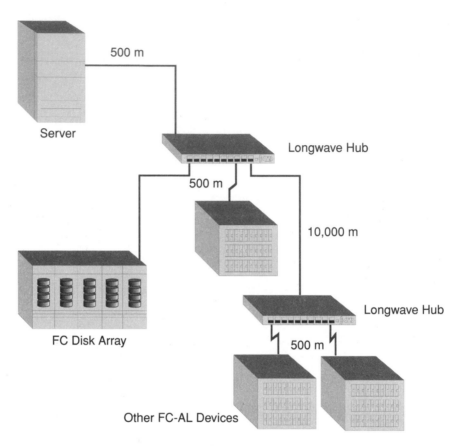

Figure 8-11   Cascaded Longwave Hub Topology

When distance is a necessity, up to two HP FC-AL hubs can be cascaded, allowing greater connectivity distances between servers and storage devices, and further increasing the breadth of deployment options. For example, cascading two shortwave hubs allows distances of up to 1.5 km. And cascading two long-wave hubs gives distances of up to 10 km, when attached to an HP-UX server. An additional 500 m can be added between the server and storage devices on either end of the hubs. This can add an additional 1,000 m to the whole SAN topology, for a maximum distance of 11 km.

The throughput and distance of Fibre Channel technology translate into increased flexibility for today's storage area networks, online transaction processing applications, and other installations where data availability and reliability are mission critical. With FC-AL hubs, campus and metropolitan SANs can be set up in widely separated nodes and still provide mirrored failover disaster recovery at gigabit speeds.

8.3.4 Fibre Channel Manager

Hewlett-Packard's Fibre Channel Manager is a device manager for the FC-AL hub. The tool is used for configuration, monitoring, and troubleshooting.

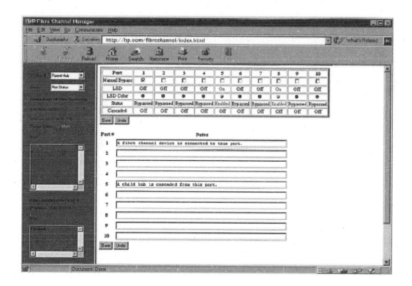

Figure 8-12   Fibre Channel Manager in Web Browser

HP Fibre Channel Manager (FCM) is a client/server intranet application, installed on a machine designated as a management server. This machine monitors any hub connected to it, whether directly or as part of a cascaded chain. FCM uses a Web server to collect, store, and present data to the client (the machine designed as the management workstation). The management workstation employs an easy-to-use Web browser to view data presented by the server.

8.3.5 Plan the FC-AL Connections

The hub does not require drivers or specific versions of the HP-UX operating system, but FC-AL devices that connect to the hub do. Contact an HP sales representative for information on hardware and software requirements for the FC-AL devices you plan to connect to the hub.

1. Verify the loop cabling configuration is correct by comparing it to the cabling example in Section 8.3.5.1. Modify the network cabling map as needed.

    Note: Incorrect wiring can lead to problems such as devices left off the loop and inaccessible by the server. Follow the guidelines below before starting.

2. Review the user-assigned loop ID (hardware address) of every FC-AL device to be connected to the hub and make sure that each ID is unique. Duplicate IDs on the loop can cause problems. In addition, each device has its own factory-assigned unique worldwide name.

3. Verify the connections between the hub port and the FC-AL mass storage device or the FC-AL host bus adapter are of the same wave type and speed. For example, plan to connect a port on the hub to a short-wave FC-AL device.

4. Document the planned connections in a cabling map.

8.3.5.1 Correct Cabling Examples

In a cascaded hub configuration, connect any port on the first hub to any port on the second hub. The following example includes all 18 nodes in the loop formed by FC-AL Device 1, Hub A, Hub B, and FC-AL Device 2. FC-AL Device 1 is connected to Port 1 on Hub A; Port 10 of Hub A connects to Port 1 of Hub B, and Port 10 on Hub B connects to FC-AL Device 2. In this configuration, Port 10 on Hub B can connect to any FC-AL device. This is just one example of cascaded hubs. The connection between hubs can occupy any combination of ports.

Hub A   Hub B

FC-AL   FC-AL

Figure 8-13   Cascaded Shortwave FC-AL Hub Configuration

8.3.5.2   Incorrect Cabling Examples

Figures 8-14 through 8-16 are examples of incorrect cabling. For example: Do not cable together two ports on the same hub. Ports between the two connections will be eliminated from the loop.

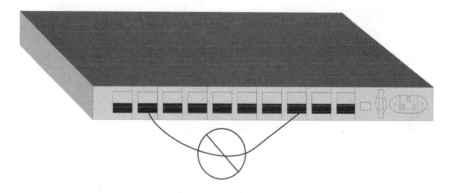

Figure 8-14   Connected Ports on the Same Hub

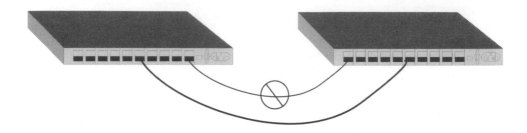

Figure 8-15   Multiple Connections Between Hubs

Do not attach more than one cable between any two hubs.

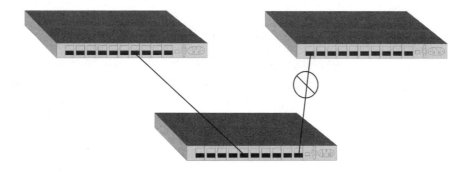

Figure 8-16   More than Two Hubs Connected

Do not attempt to connect a hub to more than one other hub.

8.4 Disk Arrays

8.4.1 HP SureStore E Disk Array FC30

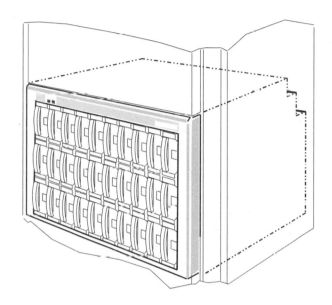

Figure 8-17 A3661A FC30 Disk Array

This Fibre Channel peripheral has substantial storage capacity. It holds up to 30 disk modules. Hewlett-Packard's highest capacity point is 18 gigabytes per disk module. This will increase with future releases. This disk array was designed specifically for use in Fibre Channel topologies.

It is a High Availability (HA) device because it employs redundant components such as:

- disk modules
- power supplies
- controller units or storage processors (SP)

It is supported by the K-, D-, T- (600 only), and V-Class Hewlett-Packard Enterprise Servers running HP-UX 10.20 TFC or later. It has a 1.063 gigabit per second optical Fibre Channel link speed, and Fibre Channel Arbitrated Loop (FC-AL) topology is also supported.

8.4.2 HP SureStore E Disk Array FC60

Figure 8-18   A5277A FC60 Disk Array

Hewlett-Packard's SureStore E Disk Array FC60 is designed to deliver a large volume of high-performance, high-availability disk storage. The Disk Array FC60 combines Fibre Channel speed, RAID protection, and multidrive capacity.

The Disk Array FC60 is five times faster than previous storage solutions and holds twice as much data.

8.4.2.1 Features and Benefits

- Fibre Channel communication for speed and reliability
- Modular construction for flexibility of configuration
- Expandable storage for capacity up to 1 TB
- High throughput
- User-configurable RAID
- 10,000-rpm disk speed

- 120-hour battery backup of cache for data safety
- Hot-swappable components for minimal service interruption

8.4.2.2 RAID

The Array Manager 60 management software lets you choose the important RAID parameters specifically to suit the environment. You can set the partition size and RAID levels, using either the graphical interface for easy selection or the scriptable command line interface that automates management of large numbers of disk arrays. You can configure the system for maximum availability and continued peak performance in the event of a disk failure. This yields a disk subsystem with a high degree of performance and predictability, regardless of activity elsewhere in the system. Or you can configure for maximum storage capacity with minimum expense.

8.4.2.3 I/O-Intensive Applications

The high-speed disks in the Disk Array FC60 rotate at 10,000 rpm, enhancing I/O performance, especially in computing applications that involve large numbers of small data transfers. This makes the Disk Array FC60 a good choice for use in I/O-intensive applications: data warehousing, OLTP, ERP, and file serving.

8.4.2.4 Internal Batteries

As with any HA installation, an uninterruptible power supply is recommended for use with the Disk Array FC60. However, internal batteries in the disk array maintain information in the controller cache for up to 120 hours. This assures no data loss even in the event of a complete loss of electrical power over a long weekend.

8.4.2.5 Zero-Downtime Maintenance

All data in the Disk Array FC60 is RAID-configured, so if any drive fails, no data is lost and system operation continues with no interruption. Power supplies and fans are redundant, so the system continues to operate even if one fails. Moreover, array controllers, disk drives, power supplies, fans, and batteries are all hot-swappable, so repairs won't affect the system's high availability.

8.4.2.6 Throughput

The FC60 has a peak throughput of 100 MBps on each channel, and sequential transfer rates of up to 200 MBps for dual controller configurations. (Although actual performance will vary depending on the application and the server environment, the FC60 has achieved actual measured performance as high as 170 MBps in the laboratory, and 130 to 170 MBps for a variety of real-world configurations.)

8.4.2.7 Scalability

The FC60 is designed to be extremely flexible. You can begin with a small amount of storage and augment it as the need for capacity grows.

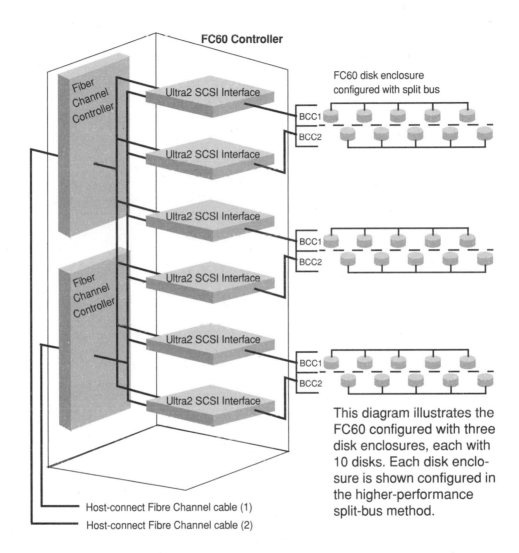

FC60 Controller

Fiber Channel Controller

Ultra2 SCSI Interface

Ultra2 SCSI Interface

Ultra2 SCSI Interface

Ultra2 SCSI Interface

Fiber Channel Controller

Ultra2 SCSI Interface

Ultra2 SCSI Interface

FC60 disk enclosure configured with split bus

BCC1
BCC2

BCC1
BCC2

BCC1
BCC2

This diagram illustrates the FC60 configured with three disk enclosures, each with 10 disks. Each disk enclosure is shown configured in the higher-performance split-bus method.

Host-connect Fibre Channel cable (1)
Host-connect Fibre Channel cable (2)

Figure 8-19   Block Diagram of the FC60

The Disk Array FC60 consists of a controller enclosure and up to six disk enclosures, all of which can be mounted in standard 19" computer equipment racks. The controller enclosure holds one or two array controllers, each with 256 megabytes of cache memory. The controller enclosure is connected to each of the disk enclosures by way of one or two Ultra2 SCSI cables.

Each disk enclosure can hold up to 10 disk drives, which can be either 9.1-or 18.2-gigabyte models. With a full complement of 18.2-gigabyte drives, a single Disk Array FC60 can provide more than 1 TB of data storage.

8.4.3 HP SureStore E Disk Array XP256

The HP SureStore E Disk Array XP256 provides high-capacity, high-speed mass storage, with continuous data availability, ease of service, scalability, and connectivity.

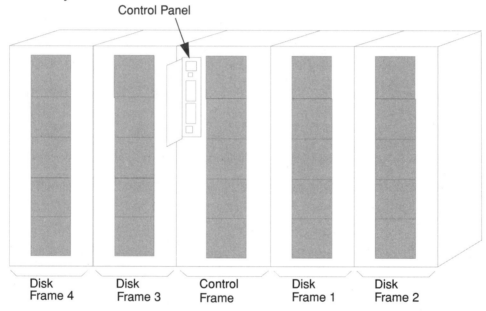

Figure 8-20   The XP256 Disk Array

The XP256 disk array can be attached to multiple open-system environments such as HP-UX, Windows NT, Solaris, AIX, etc. The disk array is designed to handle very large databases, data warehousing applications, and data mining applications.

This disk array can have up to 32 SCSI ports. It also supports Fibre Channel connections with data transfer rates of up to 100 MBps. Each Fibre Channel channel adapter (CA) supports up to 16 Fibre Channel ports. This makes the disk array ideal for clustered configurations of open-system servers.

8.4.4 Features

8.4.4.1 Continuous Data Availability

The disk array is the first RAID disk array to provide truly continuous data availability. It is designed for nonstop operation and continuous access to all user data. The disk array has no single point of component failure. It is not expected to fail in any way that would interrupt user access to data.

The disk array has component and function redundancy, providing full fault-tolerance for disk array microprocessors, control storage, control and data buses, power supplies, and cooling fans. The disk array can sustain multiple component failures and still continue to provide full access to stored data.

While access to user data is never compromised, the failure of a key component can degrade disk array performance.

8.4.4.2 Nondisruptive Service and Upgrades

Monitoring software detects failed disk drives and notifies the HP support center automatically so a service representative can replace the disk drive.

All hardware subassemblies can be removed, serviced, repaired, or replaced nondisruptively during disk array operation. All microcode upgrades can be performed during normal disk array operations, using the array's built-in service processor (SVP) or the facilities of the host. Alternate pathing can be achieved by host fail-over software and/or alternate SCSI paths. The disk array provides up to 32 SCSI ports to accommodate alternate pathing for attachment to a host.

8.4.4.3 Connectivity

SCSI Connectivity. The disk array can be configured with up to four pairs of Ultra-SCSI four-port adapters for a total of 32 ports. Each adapter provides four concurrent data transfers at rates of up to 40 MBps, for a total data transfer rate of 160 MBps. Each SCSI port can support up to 15 SCSI target IDs (TIDs), and each SCSI TID can address eight logical units (LUNs), for a total of 120 LUNs per SCSI port.

Fibre Channel Connectivity. A disk array can be configured with a maximum of four channel adapters which can each support 16 Fibre Channel ports. Each port is assigned a unique TID and can support eight LUNs. The disk array can support up to 128 LUNs attached through Fibre Channel. Fibre Channel provides data transfer rates up to 100 MBps. The disk array can support Fibre Channel Arbitrated Loop (FC-AL) and fabric topologies.

8.4.4.4   Scalability

The nonvolatile cache can also be configured from 4 GB to 16 GB in 1 GB increments. The disk array's storage capacity can be increased from 17 GB to a maximum of 9.0 TB. Disk drive and cache upgrades can be performed without interrupting user access to data and with minimal impact on the performance of the disk array.

8.4.5   Physical Components

The disk array consists of the following major hardware components:

- *One Disk Control frame.* The controller cabinet contains the control panel, Fibre Channel connection hardware, SCSI connection hardware, service processor (SVP), and control components for the disk array.

- *One to four Disk Array frames.* These cabinets contain the disk drives.

- *One service processor (SVP).* The SVP is an internally mounted laptop computer used for maintenance. It is located in the controller cabinet. The SVP is used by an HP service representative.

- *One optional remote console (RC) PC.* The remote console PC is attached to the disk array by an internal local area network (LAN). The remote console PC runs applications that monitor and manage disk array operations.

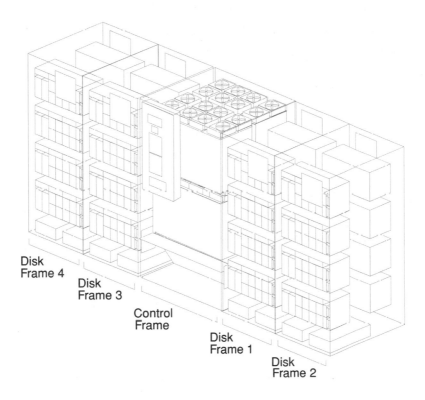

Disk
Frame 4
    Disk
    Frame 3
        Control
        Frame
            Disk
            Frame 1
                Disk
                Frame 2

Figure 8-21   XP256 Disk Array Components

8.4.5.1   Disk Control Frame

The key features and components of the disk control frame are redundant controllers and redundant power supplies. There is no active single point of failure. All control frame components can be repaired or replaced without interrupting access to user data.

8.4.5.2   Disk Array Frame

The disk array frames contain the physical disk drives, including the disk groups and the dynamic spare disk drives. The disk array can be configured with up to four disk cabinets to provide a maximum storage capacity of 9.0 TB. One disk array frame is required. The second, third, and fourth frames are optional. The first and second disk array frames are attached to the right side of the control frame. The third and fourth are attached to the left side of the control frame.

The disk array uses 3.5-inch disk drives, with a variety of available capacity points. Disk drives can be replaced without disrupting user activity. The disk array uses diagnostic and dynamic scrubbing techniques that detect and correct disk errors.

For both RAID-5 and RAID-1 array groups, any spare disk drive can back up any other disk drive of the same capacity, anywhere in the disk array, even if the failed disk and the spare disk are in different array domains. The disk array can be configured with a minimum of one and a maximum of 16 spare disk drives.

8.4.5.3   Service Processor (SVP)

The disk array comes with a built-in laptop-style PC called the service processor (SVP). The SVP is integrated into the control frame and is used only by an HP service representative.

The SVP is used to configure, maintain, and upgrade the disk array. The SVP also collects performance data for key components of the disk array for diagnostic testing and analysis. The SVP does not have access to any user data stored on the disk array.

8.4.5.4   Remote Console PC

The remote console PC runs a main remote control application and other standard and optional software to manage and monitor the disk array. The remote console PC is connected to one or more disk arrays (up to 8) using a special LAN, separate from the regular LAN.

The specific hardware requirements for the remote console PC (processor speed, storage capacity, memory) will vary depending on the optional software to be used and the number of disk arrays to be attached.

The Remote Control software for the remote console PC does not have access to any user data stored on the disk array.

8.4.6 Monitoring and Reporting

The disk array has a maintenance support application that monitors the operation of the disk array at all times, collects hardware status and error data, and transmits this data through a modem to the HP support center.

The support center analyzes the data and implements corrective action, if necessary. In the unlikely event of a component failure, the maintenance support application calls the support center immediately to report the failure. This automatic error/failure detection and reporting does not require any action on the part of the user.

In this way most disk array problems can be identified and fixed prior to actual failure. With the redundancy features of the disk array, it will remain operational even if one or more components fail.

The maintenance support application requires a dedicated telephone line. The maintenance support application does not have access to any user data stored on the disk array.

8.4.7 Optional Software

HP provides a number of optional software applications to increase data accessibility and enable continuous user data access.

8.4.7.1 HP SureStore E Performance Manager XP

HP SureStore E Performance Manager XP (PMXP) is an optional performance and usage monitoring application for the disk array. PMXP runs on the remote console PC and can monitor as many as eight disk arrays on the disk array internal LAN. PMXP monitors hardware performance, cache statistics, and I/O statistics of the attached disk arrays and displays real-time and historical data as graphs.

8.4.7.2   HP SureStore E Remote Control XP

HP SureStore E Remote Control XP is an optional software application that runs on the remote console PC. It has a primary function of reporting Remote System Information Messages (R-SIMs). In addition, it is the base software that allows a number of additional optional packages to run.

Those packages include the following:

HP SureStore E LUN Configuration Manager XP. The HP SureStore E LUN Configuration Manager XP allows open-system users to define SCSI paths, define the SCSI/FC-to-logical device (LDEV) mapping for all LUNs, and configure arbitrated-loop and fabric FC topologies. It also allows users to create "expanded-size" LUNs, permitting host access to the data on the disk array using fewer logical units.

SNMP. The Microsoft simple network management protocol (SNMP) is a part of the TCP/IP protocol suite that supports maintenance functions for the disk arrays. SNMP transfers management information and R-SIMs between the SNMP manager (on the open-system server) and the SNMP agent (on the remote console PC). The SNMP agent performs error reporting operations requested by the SNMP manager, for up to eight disk array models.

HP SureStore E Cache LUN XP. This application allows users to place data in and remove data from cache to improve disk array performance when the system accesses frequently used data.

HP SureStore E Cache LUN XP enables users to store specific high-usage data in cache memory. Cache-resident data is available at host data transfer speeds for both read and write operations. HP SureStore E Cache LUN XP can be used in conjunction with custom volume size (CVS) to provide even higher data access performance than when either of these features is used individually.

Custom Volume Size (CVS). Custom Volume Size allows the user to configure custom-size volumes (CVs), which are smaller than normal volumes. CVS improves data access performance by reducing logical device contention, as well as host I/O queue times, which can occur when several frequently accessed files are located on the same volume.

HP SureStore E Secure Manager XP. This software is for LUN security on the array. The application allows the assignment of selected LUNs to selected hosts, and hides LUNs from hosts not associated with the LUNs. HP SureStore E Secure Manager XP is executed from the remote console PC.

HP SureStore E AutoLUN XP. AutoLUN enables the optimization of data storage and retrieval on the disk array. AutoLUN monitors and provides detailed information on the physical disk drive usage of the disk array and enables you to optimize the logical volume allocation and RAID level configuration (RAID-1, RAID-5) of the disk array.

8.4.7.3   HP SureStore E Continuous Access XP

HP SureStore E Continuous Access XP enables users to copy data between disk arrays as far as 1600 km (1000 miles) apart. HP SureStore E Continuous Access XP provides synchronous and semisynchronous copy modes and can be used for data backup, disaster recovery planning, and/or data duplication. The primary LUNs are available for read and write operations during all normal remote copy operations.

8.4.7.4   HP SureStore E Business Copy XP

HP SureStore E Business Copy XP provides a quick and easy way to create an internal copy of a volume for a wide variety of purposes, such as application testing, offline backup, and Euro currency conversion testing. When used in conjunction with HP SureStore E Continuous Access XP, HP SureStore E Business Copy XP allows users to maintain multiple copies of critical data.

8.4.7.5   HP SureStore E Data Exchange XP

HP SureStore E Data Exchange XP is an optional feature of the HP Sure-Store E Disk Array XP256. It enables data stored on a multiplatform disk array (one that is connected to both a mainframe and open-system servers) to be converted and transferred between mainframe-based files and open-system files.

8.4.7.6   HP SureStore E Resource Manager XP

The HP SureStore E Resource Manager XP application allows mainframe data and open-system data to coexist in the same disk array. This reduces and optimizes storage maintenance and management overhead.

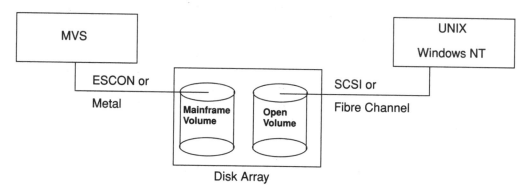

Figure 8-22   Resource Manager

8.4.7.7   HP SureStore E RAID Manager XP

This application is the host-based component of the HP SureStore E Business Copy XP and HP SureStore E Continuous Access XP applications. It gives the system administrator command line control over these programs. It is also used by HP SureStore E Continuous Access XP for local and remote host communication.

8.5 Tape Libraries

8.5.1 HP SureStore E Tape Library 20/700

Figure 8-23   HP SureStore E Tape Library 20/700

8.5.1.1 Overview

Hewlett-Packard considers the HP SureStore E Tape Library 20/700 to be the industry's most capable tape library. It has a combination of high availability, performance, and capacity. It is the tape library of choice for backing up HP's SureStore E Disk Array XP256, especially in large storage area networks.

8.5.1.2   Scalability and Speed

The tape library has a maximum capacity of up to 56 TB (assuming 2:1 compression). It can be configured with 228, 396, or 690 cartridge slots, which allows capacity to expand from 4 TB to 56 TB.

The tape library operates with high-capacity DLT8000 tape drives or high-performance HP 9840 tape drives. It supports a maximum of 20 DLT8000 tape drives, 12 HP 9840 tape drives, or a mixed combination in the same library.

The 20/700 robotics allow over 400 jobs/hour. A full audit of the library's 690 cartridges and 20 drives is two to three times faster than its competition.

8.5.1.3   High Availability

The HP SureStore E Tape Library 20/700 has hot-swappable, redundant components throughout its design, including power supplies and fans.

All serviceable parts are easily accessible, and all major components are hot-swappable and customer-serviceable with no special tools required. No lubrication or belt retensioning is ever required.

8.5.1.4   Features

- Up to 20 DLT 8000 or 12 HP 9840 drives

- 228 to 690 cartridge capacity

- 432 GB/hr maximum throughput

- 4 TB to 56 TB compressed storage capacity

- SCSI and Fibre Channel optical fiber connectivity

- Supported with HP OpenView OmniBack II and other leading storage management software

- Supported on HP-UX, Windows NT, and MPE/iX platforms

8.5.1.5   Platform, I/O Bus, and Operating System Support

UNIX

- HP 9000 Enterprise Servers:
  - A-, R-, L-, and N-Classes
  - D-, K-, T-, and V-Classes
- HP-HSC and HP-PCI
- HP-UX 10.02 and later

Windows NT

- HP NetServer LX Series: LXr, LXr Pro, LXr Pro 8
- Windows NT 4.0 Service Pack 3

MPE

- MPE/iX

8.5.2 HP SureStore E Tape Library 2/20

Figure 8-24   HP SureStore E Tape Library 2/20

This library contains one or two DLT8000 drives, a SCSI or Fibre Channel interface, remote management functionality, and a 20-tape capacity.

It is only 8.75 inches tall, and has the smallest volume of any two-drive library on the market. There are also many expansion and upgrade kits available.

Kits are available that allow the 1- or 2-drive, 20-slot library to be field upgraded to a 2- or 4-drive, 40-slot library, or a 2-, 4-, or 6-drive, 60-slot library.

HP's Remote Management option lets you obtain status and diagnostics information. You can also manage library function from a remote location by way of built-in remote management tools, or use remote management tools that integrate into leading enterprise management software.

The HP SureStore Tape Library connects with a SCSI or Fibre Channel interface. The Fibre Channel solution provides high-speed data access and long-distance connections to multiple servers sharing one or more libraries. Fibre channel technology allows you to create a LAN-free backup that eases network congestion and data-access contention inherent in LAN-based backup. SCSI-to-Fibre Channel upgrade kits are available to allow SCSI-based library customers to upgrade to Fibre Channel as their IT needs change.

8.6 SureStore E SCSI FC-SCSI FC 4/2 Bridge

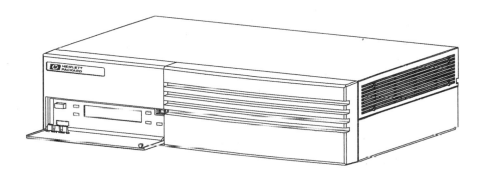

Figure 8-25   FC-SCSI 4/2 Bridge

Most data centers today are using SCSI technology. Peripheral devices are attached to their host systems through SCSI cables connected to SCSI host bus adapters (HBAs). To use Fibre Channel technology, however, each system must be able to "speak Fibre Channel." Meeting this requirement usually means expensive purchases and time-consuming conversion, migration of data, and installation of Fibre Channel-compatible hardware systems and peripherals.

Hewlett-Packard's solution to this concern is the SureStore E FC-SCSI Bridge 4/2. The bridge allows a Fibre Channel host to transmit data to SCSI devices. Using the bridge, customers can extend the distance between a host and peripherals and expand the number of SCSI devices connected to the host.

The bridge multiplexes the inputs and outputs from a single Fibre Channel connection to as many as four SCSI buses. Since each bus can support up to 15 devices, one bridge, theoretically, can support up to 60 devices (with varying levels of performance).

The advantage this device affords is to be able to attach existing SCSI devices to a Fibre Channel mass storage network.

8.6.1 Bridge Topologies

The bridge acts as a pass-through device that receives and transmits Fibre Channel packets. The host passes packets to SCSI devices as if the bridge were just another device along the path. Figure 8-26 shows a typical connection of two DLT tape libraries to a host.

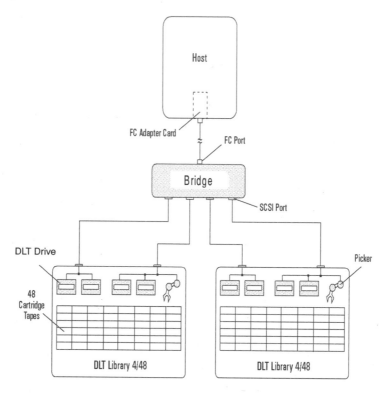

Figure 8-26   Bridge Topology with Two DLT Libraries

The product takes advantage of Fibre Channel's ability to encapsulate SCSI protocol to allow a host with an FC host bus adapter to access SCSI peripheral devices transparently over a Fibre Channel connection.

Figure 8-27 shows a host attached to four SCSI disk arrays.

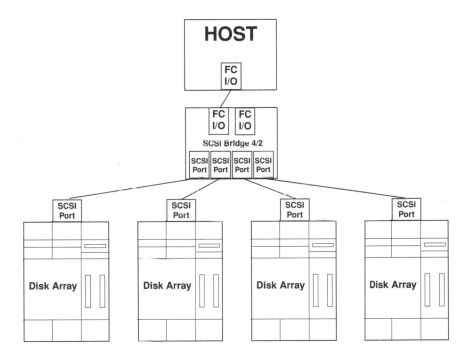

Figure 8-27   Bridge Topology with Four SCSI Disk Arrays

Another topology can be developed by adding a hub between the host and the bridge. This topology will allow an increased distance between the host and the target devices over that of the distance afforded by just incorporating a bridge.

For example, the distance from the host to a bridge can be up to 500 meters. Then the distance from the bridge to the SCSI devices can be up to 25 meters. However, by inserting a hub between the host and the bridge, an additional 500 meters can be added to the total distance.

Figure 8-28 shows a hub attached to a bridge.

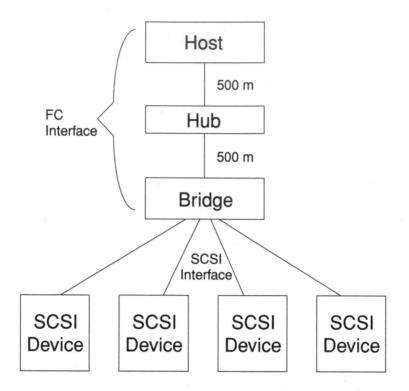

Figure 8-28   Example of a Bridge Topology with a Hub

8.7 Fibre Channel Switches

8.7.1 Brocade Silkworm 2800 Switch

Hewlett-Packard resells the Brocade SilkWorm 2800 Fibre Channel Fabric Switch. This is a high-performance 16-port fabric switch. Its high-availability features include redundant fans and optional redundant hot-swappable power supplies. The Gigabit Interface Converters are hot-swappable, as well.

The switch's ports automatically determine the port type: point-to-point, loop, or Inter-Switch Link (ISL). Switches can be cascaded, and the architecture allows for up to 239 switches in the fabric. The certified maximum is 32 switches over seven hops.

Supported GBIC types are shortwave, longwave, and passive copper.

The switch can be managed by SAN Manager DM, SNMP, Telnet, or Brocade's optional Brocade Web Tools. You can connect to it for management by means of an RJ-45 Ethernet connection or inline, over a Fibre Channel link.

8.7.2 HP Switch F16

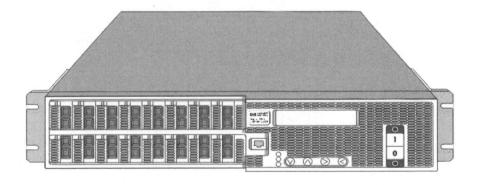

Figure 8-29   Hewlett-Packard Switch F16

The Hewlett-Packard SureStore E Switch F16 is a 16-port fabric switch. Its high-availability features include redundant power supplies and fans. The fan cage is hot-swappable.

The switch allows Fibre Channel connections to either private or public arbitrated loops or to a Fibre Channel fabric. The EPL (Enhanced Private Loop) feature is supported on HP-UX 11.0 and HP-UX 10.20 with the appropriate patches. This mode is used to allow a legacy private loop device to be attached to a fabric but operate as if it were still in a Private Loop Direct Attach (PLDA) environment. This provides connection transparency between legacy devices and the fabric.

The switch can be used to connect 16 Fibre Channel devices together. Devices may be either a direct attachment to the switch (as in a host system, or a Fibre Channel peripheral); or may be through an FC-AL Hub (provides a local loop at that particular attachment); or by way of a bridge for connecting SCSI tape or disk configurations.

The switch is fully compatible with HP's Hub L10, Hub S10, and Bridge FC 4/2. The switch supports legacy systems, such as K-Class, D-Class, T-Class, and V-Class, running the above-mentioned HP-UX 10.20 or 11.0 operating system versions. The host systems use the A3404A, A3636A, A3591B, A3740A, and A5158A Fibre Channel host bus adapters.

The switch is delivered with one G_Port card for cascading with other switches. The unit ships with no GBICs (GigaBit Interface Converters) installed. From one to four GBIC options may be used, but at least one must be ordered. Each GBIC option provides four GBICs, which are installed into any desired empty position in the switch. It is possible to use either shortwave or longwave GBIC optics. No more than one longwave option may be used at this time.

Only one loop connection may be used per Hub. There is a limit of one loop master per Fabric Port. If more than one loop master (FL_Port) is used, one will remain inactive until such time as the first FL_Port fails.

The switch operates as a full-bandwidth crosspoint connection device, capable of providing up to eight concurrent connections. Each connection operates at full 1 Gbps speed. This is a significant improvement over a loop configuration, which has a total speed of 1 Gbps, but is a shared polling environment.

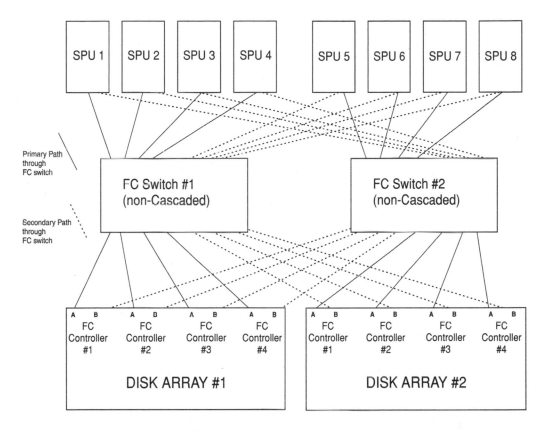

Figure 8-30   FC Switch Configuration

The Gigabit Fibre Channel Switch supports no more than two uncascaded switches per cluster/configuration. There may be no more than eight hosts per pair of switch connections. This allows for a High Availability (HA) redundant path configuration to maximize the availability of the host systems and mass storage. See Figure 8-30.

The switch can be managed through SAN Manager (DM), Fibre Channel Manager, and Storage Node Manager.

An Interview with Duane Zitzner

We asked Duane Zitzner, a senior HP executive, to answer our questions about HP's positioning and commitment to SAN technology.

We've documented HP hardware and software products for years, and that has given us a practical, but only informal, sense of how HP is evolving and where HP products are going. However, it doesn't provide a high-level view of corporate strategy. We wanted to learn where Hewlett-Packard Company would position itself in the current SAN storage revolution, so we found the perfect person to ask.

9.1 Biography

Duane E. Zitzner is president of Hewlett-Packard Company's Computing Systems. He is responsible for computer products and systems, including commercial and home PCs, HP NetServers, UNIX servers, storage, and software products such as OpenView. Zitzner also manages HP's investments in computer technology, and ensures proper resource allocation for the entire Computing Systems segment. In addition, he is an elected HP vice president and a member of the Executive Council. Zitzner is based in Cupertino, California.

Zitzner joined HP in 1989 as a section manager in the Roseville Networks Division in California. In 1990, he was promoted to research-and-development manager of the Network Architecture Lab, and in 1991, he was named general manager of the California PC Division, which became the Network Server Division in 1993. He was named general manager of the Networked Systems Business Unit in 1994, was promoted to general manager of the Personal Information Products Group in 1996, and later that year was elected an HP vice president. He continued as vice president and general manager when PSG became a group within the Computer Organization in 1997, and was named president of Computing Systems in 1999.

Before joining HP, Zitzner held various management and technical jobs in software and architecture at IBM. Previous to that, he was a programmer at Univac.

Zitzner holds a bachelor's degree in mathematics from the University of Wisconsin in Madison, and he completed graduate studies in computer science at the University of Minnesota in Minneapolis.[1]

---

1.   From the official Hewlett-Packard biography.

9.2 Interview

Q. Hewlett-Packard's stock has done very well in recent months. To what extent do HP's mass storage products (and Storage Area Network products in particular) contribute to the company's success?

A. Hewlett-Packard is one of the leading storage vendors in the world, and HP has identified storage as a strategic growth area for the company. Storage is a multibillion dollar business for HP, and is therefore expected to significantly contribute to the company's success. HP has demonstrated its belief and commitment to storage networking by offering a broad portfolio of Storage Area Network (SAN), Network Attached Storage (NAS), and storage management software products and solutions.

Q. You must see HP as a leader in the development of Storage Area Network technology. For example, HP is a member of the Fibre Channel Industry Association and a joint developer of Linear Tape-Open technology. What is HP doing to maintain its lead in SAN products?

A. HP intends to maintain its leadership position by staying close to customers, to provide solutions to today's problems and tomorrow's opportunities. HP has a product and solution investment strategy that aligns with this objective. As a leader in open systems, HP has the experience and capability to continue to deliver leading SAN products and solutions.

Q. HP has introduced a number of products that work well in SANs, in particular the XP256 disk array and the 20/700 tape library. In general, what HP products will be launched to meet the future needs of the SAN customer?

A. In May 1999, HP made a bold statement to the market regarding its view of the future. HP announced the HP Equation Architecture: the vision of an open pool of storage, safely and efficiently providing 100% data availability and infinite scalability. Since that time, HP has regularly announced new products, solutions, and services that support this vision. These include multiple operating system support for products, storage management software for SANs, and storage consolidation solutions across the

SAN for Windows NT environments. Customers rely on HP to continue to drive toward open SANs, and HP will continue to deliver.

Q. *HP's vision is to be an enabler of e-business by providing e-commerce solutions. Where does the Storage Area Network fit in your vision of HP's leadership in e-commerce?*

A. HP has been a leading driver of the next chapter of the Internet. This is a world where the Internet works for you in ways that were unimaginable only a short time ago. The Internet, e-business, e-commerce, and the new world of e-services is a networked world. Storage will become even more crucial as online data becomes commonplace. Storage Area Networks fit into that vision very well, because SANs provide the networked storage environment that provides the performance, availability, connectivity, scalability, and security that is required.

Q. *InfoStor magazine predicts that the year 2000 will be the Year of the SAN. Will HP be the leader in SAN development? If so, how?*

A. HP intends to lead the storage industry into the next generation of Web-enabled storage network solutions. This includes both NAS and SANs. While HP does not discuss unreleased products, the company has a proven track record of leading in SANs and expects to continue to do so through the ongoing development and introduction of new products, solutions, and services.

CHAPTER 10

Future Developments

This chapter discusses:

- **What drives change?**
- **SAN technology developments**
- **Technology changes outside the SAN**
- **New IT applications**
- **The IT SAN management professional**
- **Future applications**
- **The final word**

SAN technology is evolving at a rapid pace. This chapter describes future SAN developments and possible applications.

Someone once said, "Study the future, because you're going to spend the rest of your life there." This would be a relatively easy task if the future stayed comfortably in the future, but it has a nasty habit of becoming the present faster than we can anticipate.

As a case in point, in Spring 2000, Celera Genomics announced that it had finished decoding the entire DNA map for an individual, a major milestone. Craig Venter, the president of Celera, pointed out that the privately funded project was well ahead of the federally funded Human Genome Project, which is scheduled for completion in 2003 or 2005 (sources vary on the year). Venter said supercomputers were used to analyze the information, and Celera would finish the work in a few weeks.

"In a few weeks" came just 12 weeks later, as this book was being prepared for the printer. At a news conference, called by the President of the United States and attended (via satellite link) by British Prime Minister Tony Blair, Venter announced 99% completion, having sequenced 3.21 billion of the 3.5 billion chemical letters of the human genome.

The point is, the biggest breakthrough ever in biotechnology, disease eradication, and extension of human life happened years before it was predicted. Did computers and mass storage help this to happen?

Yes. It should come as no surprise to IT professionals that progress on sequencing, analyzing, and annotating the human genome requires a supercomputer and significant storage resources. In an interview on PBS television in April, Venter explained that the work had already consumed 80 TB of storage. It appears that this breakthrough would not have been possible without mass storage of tremendous scale—exactly the scale of storage available through Storage Area Networks.

The human genome project, the first great technological breakthrough of the 21st century, is just the sort of thing the SAN makes possible. With this achievement as inspiration, let's look ahead to where SANs (and technology in general) are progressing.

10.1 What Drives Change?

Change happens. Why?

It is a given that necessity is the mother of invention. Need drives change; but paradoxically, when we have achieved change, we suddenly determine that we have new needs. It may be that invention is the mother of necessity.

It wasn't that long ago that a telephone was a luxury in an American home. The photocopier (an invention turned down by some of the biggest corporations in the United States because it "wasn't needed") was a curiosity. To the list of past oddities and "nice to have" devices, add the fax machine, the microwave oven, the pocket calculator, and even the personal computer. Now these items are considered indispensable.

The SAN is beginning its journey from "promising" to "indispensable." The SAN is the optimal solution to burgeoning mass storage needs, but once those needs are met, more demanding mass storage needs will emerge to drive SAN development.

Can we estimate the rate of change accurately? No. Futurists point out that it's a human trait to predict change conservatively. We look at change linearly, but it always takes place exponentially. Change can go even faster because of technology discontinuities or "jumps"—the sudden appearance of radical new technologies.

Even as this book was developed, we read new announcements about LTO tape technology and articles about 2 GB Fibre Channel. And about the only prediction people have gotten right is the speed of microprocessors in PCs doubling about every 18 months. The 5.4 MHz 8088 you owned in 1984 is now a machine with a 733 MHz CPU.

Since the rate of technology changes cannot be predicted with any great accuracy, and are typically too conservative, we're prepared to predict aggressively, running the risk of hitting a little wide of the mark.

The useful applications derived from a new technology, and their social impacts, are rarely predicted with accuracy. In the 1950s, visionaries predicted personal flying machines in every garage, but didn't mention the personal computer. They missed on both counts. Even Tim Berners-Lee, the British programmer credited with inventing the World Wide Web, admits the WWW has turned out to be quite a different thing than the entity he envisioned.

Therefore, this chapter is based on beliefs, desires, and hopes as much as extrapolations of existing fact. We can tell you some of the trends, but the future implementations of SAN technology are dependent on how we all view technology and people.

We believe that people are essentially good, and will almost always do good. We also consider technology to be a good thing, an enabler for people to do better and get more out of life.

Will the SAN makes things better? It will make things happen, but who can say better? We'd like to think so. Given that, let's launch into speculation about the future.

10.2 SAN Technology Developments

The SAN will not go the way of the 5.25" diskette. It is a robust, modular, scalable architecture. The SAN will respond to the two great, inevitable drivers of high technology: "more" and "faster." A wonderful new driver is "easier."

10.2.1 Speed

Faster, faster, faster. As mentioned earlier in this book, 2 Gbps Fibre Channel will earn end-user acceptance this year. In plain terms, as soon as manufacturers offer it, customers will buy it. This is startling, considering that 1 Gbps Fibre Channel is just growing in acceptance. Recall that 4 Gbps Fibre Channel is part of the ANSI standard, so can it be far behind? However, even at 2 Gbps some applications (such as moving uncompressed high-definition television data) become viable.

10.2.2 Distance

More distance, more distance, more distance. The SAN can reach greater distances in businesses and on campuses than SCSI. The fiber optic medium is relatively cheap and easy to install, so why shouldn't enterprises look for distance solutions to a variety of problems? If the speed of the FC connection will double or quadruple, do delays caused by distance really make a difference?

If you assume that fiber optic cable is no more difficult or expensive to lay than other connection media, then businesses, government, and schools can get more life out of existing buildings by expanding their interfloor and interbuilding links.

As telephone companies lay more fiber optic cable, businesses will take advantage of it for purposes of connecting to cross-town operations.

Further, nothing happens in a vacuum. Changes in distance and speed of data delivery over fiber will help drive changes to T-1, OC-3, and OC-12 wide area connection technology.

What are the social consequences of faster access over longer distances? Businesses, always conscious of the high price of real estate, might take two paths. First, they could locate data centers in declining urban districts, save some rent money, and help revitalize the neighborhood, too. The land is cheaper, the buildings are cheaper, and there's potentially no degradation in performance. Alternately, businesses might locate data centers on the prairies or in the foothills, helping those local economies. They'd also be located "away from the fault line," as those of us from earthquake-prone Los Angeles or Silicon Valley might say.

10.2.3 Capacity

More capacity, more capacity, more capacity. It is the eternal cry of commercial Information Technology.

HP's disk capacity point, *at this moment*, is 47 GB, but that's just a passing figure. Higher-capacity disk drives with small form factors will continue to come. We would expect to see drives in the 100 GB range within a year, with more than 500 drives in large disk arrays.

The IT world abhors unused capacity, so as increased storage capacity becomes available, it will fill up. This will, of course, create a demand for greater capacity.

Bigger capacities for SANs will drive bigger capacities in Network Attached Storage and PCs. They will store more. Even at this moment, we know of a few PC implementations with 40+ GB of disk storage.

10.2.4 Improved Switches and Hubs

More interconnects. Switches and hubs shouldn't become the restraining component in building elaborate SANs. Given that the fabric switch is inherently more flexible than the FC-AL hub, we expect to see more switches with greater capabilities: more ports, more cascading options, more intelligence. It's inevitable that prices will come down as the number of units manufactured increases.

Hubs will not disappear. These devices will still have a place in smaller SANs, and public loops attached to switches. The hub might become a low-cost building block for implementing Fibre Channel in Small Office/Home Office (SOHO) installations.

10.2.5 Easier Connects

Your stress level as a storage management professional will be lowered as the process of connecting new devices becomes easier.

Fabric switch technology already provides for cascadable switches. There should be plenty of ways to connect new devices to a SAN, and you will never feel "strapped for ports." And we expect that switches will continue to develop good manners by discovering new devices and making them part of the fabric with a minimum of human interaction.

The worst-case scenario is that after connecting a new mass storage device, you'll simply walk over to your workstation, execute the Web-based management software, and bring the new device onto your SAN with just a few mouse clicks.

Of course (over the short term, until your operating system grows more intelligent), you'll still have to partition, create file systems, and migrate data to new devices.

10.2.6 Better Backups

When it comes to backups, in many respects, the future is here. It arrived while this book was being written, and for many of us, it didn't arrive a moment too soon. Many of the features we'd like to see in backup and restore are happening now. They include:

- *"Native" Fibre Channel tape drives*. StorageTek and Exabyte have announced tape drives that don't require a Fibre Channel/SCSI bridge to connect.

- *Denser, faster tapes*. The Ultrium Tape format and Sony DTF-2 tape have the capacity to meet tape backup needs for some years to come.

- *Bigger tape libraries*. There's a better selection of large tape library solutions than ever, although the vast majority are SCSI-based and require a bridge to connect to the SAN. There is apparently no limit to the number of drives and number of tape slots that can be integrated into a single cabinet.

- *LAN-less and serverless backup*. Hewlett-Packard's Omniback II software is the kind of utility that accomplishes this task.

- *Disk-to-disk backups*. HP's Continuous Access XP software allows you to make copies from one XP256 disk array to another XP256. HP's Business Copy XP software lets you make copies to another disk in the same XP256.

The backup picture looks pretty good at the moment. However, we'll have to see how long it takes before increased online storage puts the backup process under more pressure.

10.2.7 Easier Maintenance

Whether you are buying candy over the Internet, or lying on the operating table while your medical imaging data is being retrieved, the phrase "the computer is down" has become completely unacceptable. So it's necessary to maintain the health of the SAN as effectively as possible without stopping operations.

Fortunately, in several respects the future is here already. Consider the following factors:

- Virtually every manufacturer of SAN equipment recognizes the "fix on the fly" operational model and has made the word "robust" a component of every product announcement.

- Disk arrays have redundant fans, power supplies, and controllers. RAID technology helps overcome the problem of unavailable data caused by failed disk drives. Hot-swappable disk modules are sometimes featured.

- Other devices, such as switches, have redundant components.

- Smart hubs and switches bypass failed ports. The device may be unavailable, but the SAN continues to function.

- A product announcement for a Brocade switch cites 70 fewer parts in the current model of the device. The reasoning is that with fewer parts, there's less to break.

- Most devices report failures, using SNMP or a similar mechanism. Devices with the best manners have a "phone home" capability. The device calls the manufacturer's response center, and a customer engineer is on the way with replacement parts—sometimes before the customer knows anything has gone wrong.

- The smart SAN designer (you) has made "no single point of failure" a mantra. Every device is double-pathed. In *The Book of Five Rings*, written in 1643, Miyamoto Musashi points out, "It is better to wield two long swords rather than just one, when facing a number of opponents alone."

10.2.8 Easier Storage Management

As storage grows, we don't want storage management problems to grow. Especially, we don't want storage management stress to grow.

The goal is to eliminate the stress, as humankind prefers not to have problems bigger than its ability to manage them. We see the SAN of the future as being not more complicated to manage, but less complicated.

In this respect, the future can't get here fast enough. We expect to see a vast improvement in storage management software in just the next year.

Up to this point, there have been a number of methods for reporting problems at the device level: the ubiquitous HP-UX ioscan command, Event Monitoring Service, Storage Node Manager, and Fibre Channel Manager, just to name a few.

Complex storage devices, like HP's XP256 disk array, have a collection of monitoring and management software. The bag full of essential tools includes Logical Unit Size Expansion (LUSE) to make big LUNs, Custom Volume Size (CVS) to make little LUNs, Performance Manager XP to display graphs and adjust performance, Cache LUN to manage the cache, and Secure LUN to zone LUNs. And that's just for one device.

We expect that better and easier SAN management is on the immediate horizon. HP is justifiably proud of its SAN Manager DM and SAN Manager LM products. These applications provide broad control of key SAN elements, and once we feel comfortable with simple, comprehensive human management, we can look ahead to automated management.

AutoPath XP is a good example. This is a small application that performs automatic failover and load balancing over multiple paths. Of course, you have to define the paths, but we would expect that soon path management software will find the paths for you. Fixing a failed path will still require human intervention to replace a severed fiber optic cable or a failed GBIC.

10.2.9 Intelligent Storage

Managing today's storage is still a little like starting a Model T Ford. It takes lots of little manual operations. This is soon to be replaced by a vastly more automated approach.

The operative term for the future of storage management is "Policy Management." The simple definition: just tell the SAN what you want and it will do it for you. Ideally, those directives might be:

- "Add more storage"
- "Allocate storage where and when it's needed"
- "Manage my backups"
- "Recover my data"
- "Optimize your performance"
- "Find the best solution and tell me"
- "Find the best solution and don't tell me"

10.3 Technology Changes Outside the SAN

Changes in other sectors of Information Technology drive SAN development. To return the favor, SAN development will drive new changes in these sectors.

10.3.1 The Internet

The Internet started as a relatively small network of interconnected university and government computers, and, by extension, a network of users. Today, there are tens (some reports say hundreds) of millions of connected PCs. Its growth drives of lot of things, and it should be no surprise at all that it's a driver of SAN development.

The Internet (and the World Wide Web in particular) is a young, healthy boomtown with a brawling, frontier mentality. And that's a pretty good thing.

There's plenty of access, but not much data.

Not much data? Right. The information available on the World Wide Web is limited. Data is moving to the Web only as fast as Web pages and Portable Document Format (PDF) files can be created.

The exceptions are well-crafted databases designed to make investing, retail sales, and business-to-business (B2B) commerce work smoothly—but that's about selling things, which is not the world's only concern.

Part of the charm of today's Internet is Balkanized, disorganized, incomplete information, with links served up in erratic fashion by hundreds of search engines. However, that charm will grow a little tedious over the next few years.

As the Internet satisfies our hunger for more information, made available to us faster, it makes us hungrier for more. It drives putting more information, bigger in size and importance, online. However, we will require well-organized, meaningful information, and storing that information is a job for the SAN. When large SANs with such data are connected to the Internet, we will see technological and social changes now barely dreamed of.

10.3.2 Wireless Computing

Wireless computing is about to have a giant impact. At this point, too many palmtop computers are used simply as hand-held address books. The next phase, coming up rapidly, is where the palmtop is used as an Internet terminal with the copper phone wire removed.

Dialing in to the Internet over phone lines provides immediate access to information from a fixed location. Accessing the Internet without the constraint of a phone line will trigger a revolution in behavior. And that revolution is a driver in SAN development.

Even today, you can get an e-mail on your palmtop alerting you that your dotcom stock has gone up (or down) in value. Even today, you can surf the Web while waiting at the laundromat.

Would you like to be alerted when to take your medication? Or find the location of the nearest hospital if you forget to take it? That's going to take a serious medical database behind that Internet functionality, and there will be a SAN storing the data.

But wireless computing is hardly just about palmtops. There are vast sections of the world, and many nations, that missed the Industrial Revolution. The poorest nations in the world have few roads and fewer telephone lines, and they are too economically strapped to build that infrastructure. They cannot replicate the infrastructures of the developed nations, but with wireless computing, they won't have to.

It is already clear that a remote village can join the rest of the world with a generator, a satellite disk, a VCR, and TV monitor, all delivered by helicopter. The same thing can happen with computing power. Wireless computing and SANs will hurl emerging nations into the 21st century, and no roads or copper wires are required. In order for government, education, and commerce to work, less-developed countries must have shared data and access to it. That is obtainable only through SANs and a sophisticated wireless technology.

10.3.3 Storage Capacity

Will SANs incorporate improved storage devices that don't exist yet? Of course they will. Here is a direct quote from an IBM press release:

SAN JOSE, California. October 4, 1999—IBM has set a new computer data storage world record of 35.3 billion data bits per square inch on a magnetic hard disk—a 75 percent increase over the 20-billion-bit milestone the company achieved less than five months ago.

The press release calculates that a single 3.5" desktop drive platter would hold nearly 50 GB. And you know 3.5" drives are multiplatter affairs. As a bonus, drives with greater density are lighter, consume less energy, presumably generate less heat, and (in IBM's words) "tend to be more reliable." Also, notice that the previous density record was set only five months prior.

Even at a conservative calculation of 200 GB per drive and 500 drives in a disk array, that's 100 TB in a single enclosure!

In addition, as high-density, high-capacity drives populate desktop and laptop computers, the relationship between the user and the SAN will change. For example, even if downloading high-quality video on demand over distance in real time is not yet possible, users will be able to order tonight's movie in advance. The user would use his or her palmtop computer over a wireless connection to reach the video provider, and request tonight's feature be downloaded from a large SAN to his or her 1.5 TB storage device connected to the television.

New disk drive technologies will produce quantum jumps in capacity. Consider ferroelectric molecular holographic optical storage nanotechnology, or holographic mass storage, for short. HMS isn't a common term yet, but it could become one. Colossal Storage of Fremont, CA, holds patents on components of this technology, and suggests the technology could produce capacities of 10 TB on a 3.5" disk!

10.4 New IT Applications

Articles in Information Technology publications tease us about new uses of technology. It's wise to pay attention to them, because today's article about what's possible quickly turns into reality. There are several applications emerging now that are the logical extension of SAN technology.

10.4.1 Storage on Demand (A Utility Company)

It's great to have a lot of your own storage, but wouldn't it be useful to rent just what you need for as long as you need it? It could be a lifesaver to call the Acme Data Storage Company in the morning and say, "I need 300 GB for a month." Having worked out the connection technology in the past, you expect the storage company representative to tell you that your disk space will be available that afternoon.

For a temporary project, you could give up the rented storage as soon as it was complete. For a permanent application, you get things running at the storage company while waiting for your new 300 GB disk array to be shipped and installed.

If the price picture looks good to you, you could leave your data at the storage company permanently. Potentially, this is one of the most problem-free methods of managing mass storage.

This Storage Service Provider (SSP) is a descendant of the service bureau of the 1960s. Then, you could have your work done on the service bureau's mainframe, often delivering input and picking up output literally "over the counter."

Will enterprises trust another business to manage their data? From past history, it would seem so. Also, there's a current trend to outsource many other business functions, so why not data?

All equipment manufacturers stress that your data is an asset—an invaluable asset. Perhaps storage-on-demand vendors will promote the idea that your data is too valuable for you to store it yourself.

This line of business is evolving as we speak: the media report that SNI and StorageTek are jointly investigating storage utilities; HP and Qwest have a relationship, and so do HP and Intira.

10.4.2 The Backup Business (A Utility Company)

Since backup tends to be tedious and time consuming, why not pay an outside company to do it, or at least the parts you don't want to handle? If an IT department does site-wide automatic PC backup to, say, 1000 PCs in the division, it might want to hire the Acme Backup Company instead of using in-house resources.

In planning disaster recovery scenarios for your servers and SAN, you might find equipping and staffing a disaster recovery site to be too costly. And since you'd probably like your backup data to be vaulted off-site, what difference does it make whether you or a backup company own the equipment and do the backup?

A backup company with a good SAN might be one of the great IT profit centers of the immediate future. It would require one or two high-end disk arrays, remote mirroring, local mirroring, and two or three large tape libraries to get off to a healthy start.

10.4.3 Apps on Tap (A Utility Company)

Maybe storing data at a "foreign" site isn't appropriate for your IT department. How would you like to obtain or access your application software from an Application Service Provider?

The Application Service Provider (ASP) Industry Consortium explains that application service providers "deliver and manage applications and computer services from remote data centers to multiple users via the Internet or a private network." The group says it's cost-effective, citing savings of "33% to 53% over purchasing and managing the hardware and software" yourself. Specific details of application "rental" are not provided.

True, maintaining desktop productivity applications for large corporate sites is a burden. That burden includes keeping dozens of desktop applications at current version levels all the time, and installing software on new machines.

Any number of variations are possible. You could simply call the Acme Applications Utility Company and say, "I'd like 1000 licenses worth of Microsoft Office 2000, please." The application company sends the software to your users and the licenses to your license management database.

Some in-house operations already perform no installations. They simply notify users that new software is available for user download from the site repository. With apps on tap, the users could do the same download, but directly from the utility company. Installs and upgrades of PC software can become the vendor's concern.

Increasingly, you will hear the concept of just paying for the "amount" of an application you use. In theory, an application could execute from a remote site, just like now when applications are resident on a central onsite server. The difference is that, like your electric, gas, or telephone consumption, you'd be billed "click charges," for only the "amount" of MRP, spreadsheet, or word processing software you used.

10.4.4 Remote Management (A Utility Company)

The remote SAN management company may be the ultimate in abstract SAN applications, because the vendor doesn't need to own a SAN. Yet it's a perfectly sensible application for the near future.

Remote management of SANs may be one of the most cost-effective ways for companies to stretch their IT dollars. It begins with the idea that in many companies the central IT department already manages branch-office IT remotely. Those companies have determined that it's not cost-effective to have trained IT people at the branch offices.

Computer hardware manufacturers recognize this. For example, HP sells network appliances such as the JetDirect 4000 (a print spooler) that can be shipped directly to branch offices, where the staff merely plugs them in. Corporate IT does the rest of the configuration over the wire.

Well, then, why not move central site storage management from the IT department to a remote vendor? Simply call the Acme Remote Management Company and arrange for them to provide 24/7 monitoring and management of its data. You no longer need to maintain an excessively large central site staff, whose main job is to watch the disk drives spin.

This idea is already working for LAN management. An Irvine, CA, remote management company cited this math: they charge customers $6000/month for remote LAN management and provide 24/7 coverage. That amounts to $72,000/year, but that's less than it would cost the customer to hire one network administrator. The administrator's salary would probably be higher, and doesn't include the cost of benefits. And even so, the employee works only one shift.

There is already a sufficient number of standalone and Web-based SAN monitoring and management packages to do the job. Generally, the SAN doesn't know whether it's being managed from a workstation in the next room or from a site a thousand miles away.

10.5 The IT SAN Management Professional

At the top of *InfoStor* magazine, it says the publication provides "News and Information for Data Storage Professionals." It's a given that data storage professionals exist, but are there SAN management professionals?

Yes, indeed. And the future looks bright for those developing careers in SAN engineering. A quick search under "SAN" and "Storage Area Network" at dice.com produced 1532 matching listings.

Titles range from some non-SAN sounding ones, such as "Sr. Engineer (File Storage)," to some very SAN-centric ones, such as "Storage Area Network Architect." Two annual salaries that caught our eye were $104,000 and $120,000.

Go see for yourself. Closer examination will show that a large number of the openings are for those making SAN products: Dell, Brocade, Hewlett-Packard, etc. That's understandable. In terms of customers using SANs, one source estimates that SANs are showing themselves in only about 3% of data centers so far. That leaves a lot of data centers that will be installing SANs in the future.

A typical job description for an e-business reads:

Lead the technical development of new Storage Services using Storage Area Network (SAN) technology, for a rapidly growing Integrated Communications Provider (ICP) in the Boston area. Services to include On-Line Storage, Continuous Production, Disaster Recovery services, and other storage-centric services.

Identify new standardized services to be developed, based on an understanding of customer requirements and leveraging the capabilities of SAN technology. Develop Storage Services designs, standards, and procedures to enable services to be sold to customers and delivered in a repeatable and scalable manner. Lead development of the SAN environment in support of other E-Services (Application Hosting, B2B Commerce, ASP solutions, etc.) that rely heavily on storage as an integral part of the infrastructure.

The required experience? A BSEE or computer science degree, five years experience in data networking at a data center, and senior-level expertise in network design as it relates to Storage Area Networks.

10.6 Future Applications

If you have a long enough lever, and a fulcrum upon which to place it, you can move the world. The Storage Area Network is the lever and the Internet is the fulcrum, and there's every reason to believe that you, as a SAN professional, will move the world in the not-too-distant future.

What would happen if people had faster access to more (and better) information? There have been some important moments when information in quantity was distributed widely:

- The destruction of the library at Alexandria in 638 prompted scholars to save what books they could and flee. They spread the information throughout the Mediterranean and beyond.

- The conquest of Granada in 1492 made the science and art of the Moorish empire available to European scholars.

- In a move that did not require conquering a city or an empire, Gutenberg's development of moveable type and the printing press replicated ideas and made them available to many people.

When information in almost any field of human endeavor is distributed effectively, the world moves. In our time, the SAN is the basis for this process.

What applications can grow out of SAN technology? Let's look at a few.

10.6.1 Video on Demand

High Definition Television (HDTV) exists, but it is not yet broadcast to people's homes. The formula in the video industry is that when the price of receivers drops to $1000, people will buy them.

Even after HDTV broadcasting becomes widespread, the interest will be in video on demand. That's a world where any video, on any subject, in any language, will be available to you when you want to see it, and the storage requirements are so intense that it's clearly a SAN application.

So how "big" is HDTV? We've been advised by two video engineers that HDTV is a slippery subject to talk about, because a standard format and a standard for compression are both under debate.

But for the sake of argument, let's look at uncompressed HDTV, the highest quality available. Let's use the 1080i standard: 1080 lines, 1920 pixels, wide screen 16:9 aspect ratio, 30 frames per second, interlace scanned.

1920 pixels per line X 1080 lines X 30 frames per second X 2 bytes per pixel = 124,416,000 (124.416 MB) bytes for one second of HD video. That math suggests that a minute of HDTV requires about 7.46 GB and a 105-minute feature film requires about 783 GB. We also have a more conservative (and conflicting) calculation that yields about 1.169 TB for a feature film.

Either way, that's not an unmanageable amount of data for a SAN.

Transmitting HDTV into homes will require the video industry to agree on the compression "sweet spot," the best acceptable quality produced by the highest rate of compression. Compression is essential, because there is currently no delivery medium for homes with a bandwidth to carry 124 MBps of uncompressed video. We have heard of compression formulas to send video at rates as low as 19.6 MBps but can't confirm that the quality is acceptable. Even so, 19.6 MBps cannot realistically be sent to homes yet.

However, a solution will be found, and as HDTV video on demand becomes a reality, it will surely alter all current thinking about broadcast TV and cable television.

What about the medium carrying uncompressed HDTV? It appears that 2 GB Fibre Channel could do it. So, imagine going to the movie theatre of the future at the mall. This cineplex has 100 small viewing rooms holding up to eight people each. There's a 300 TB SAN with 2 GB Fibre Channel connections to the rooms. What's playing? Just about whatever you want, because you have 300 movies to choose from. You pay one price for your whole party for the room and go in to select whatever movie you want. You watch a high-quality image on a large screen, and you can start it, pause it, and stop it whenever you want.

For you, you get a new kind of social, customized, entertainment experience. And the movie operator saves money in many ways: no scheduling problems; savings in advertising; no full houses requiring viewers to be turned away; no half-filled houses; no calculation of the number of screens to put a new feature on; additional revenues from old favorites; and no worries about booking a film for too short or too long a time period. Of course the "films" aren't films anymore, and they're downloaded from the distributor directly into the movie operator's SAN.

10.6.2 Education

Bringing the Internet into every classroom in America sounded like a noble idea when it was first floated, but has evolved into a phrase used by politicians to show that they're interested in education and have some clue about technology. Having the Internet in classrooms is still a great idea, but it's only a start. Students also need content, and that content resides in well-crafted, formal, up-to-date textbooks.

When school districts share large SANs, there's a potential for putting every available textbook online. Those texts will be served to schools, and will be printable or accessible online.

That means the day of the expensive textbook is over, and school districts with tight budgets will welcome that. There's no budget-driven limitation on choice either. A teacher won't be limited to just one text or old texts; he or she will be able to choose from a variety of textbooks for the same class.

The reason secondary and college texts cost so much is simple: too complex a document bought by too few school districts or college students. With electronic books stored on a SAN and worldwide distribution, excellent textbooks will be within everyone's reach.

Even today, teachers can build custom video lessons by selecting stock still pictures and full motion video from video disks and assembling a sequence on VHS tape. With large SANs, teachers will have a much wider choice of such materials and will be able to easily create videotapes, CDs, and DVDs. Instead of a hodgepodge of specialized equipment, only a PC will be required.

The SAN has scalability, distance, and speed; so schools in different school districts can share learning data. Multiple school districts can share the costs of data on tap from central knowlege supply organizations.

10.6.3 Government that Works for People

The United States government has been called the world's largest publisher. In addition, it may have the world's largest collection of unintegrated data. That data falls into two grand categories: general information you can use, and specific information about you.

Even in the 21st century, access to government records and other information is inefficient and tedious. States and counties don't do a particularly better job. Government computers and storage are likely to be older and inadequate.

Imagine government with large SANs and well-managed data. We might see government that works better to serve the people.

It was too long in coming, but at last we can download tax forms and instructions electronically, and the Internal Revenue Service encourages electronic filing. That's fine, but wouldn't it be handy to look at your personal income tax data from past years, along with your Social Security data, Veterans Administration data, and Immigration and Naturalization Service data?

On the state and county level, it would be convenient to see your voter registration, automobile registration, assessor's information for your house, business license record, etc.

The data is there, but it's not integrated and it's not accessible. With a SAN and the Internet, that will all change. And when you can see and update your government data, you will exercise a greater level of control over it.

Unfortunately, information is power, and where there is power, there is sometimes abuse. If too much information about people is concentrated in one place, there's a serious risk of loss of privacy. What are the dangers of government collecting too much data about individuals in a well-integrated database?

If we assume a population in the United States of about 270 million people and dedicate 1 MB of storage for each person's data, it would only take 270 TB to create a dossier for every individual in the country. Would that be a good thing?

10.6.4 Medicine

The biggest threat to getting quality health care in the United States is by no means the quality of the doctors, hospitals, or pharmaceuticals. It's the paperwork. In a recent National Public Radio interview, a doctor explained that in a 13-hour workday, she spent three to four hours filling out pieces of paper.

Every time you change doctors, you are asked to complete a new health history, providing the same information on new pieces of paper. Your chart is updated manually by the doctor during a visit. What's even more startling is that your electrocardiogram and X-rays are separate documents that can get separated from your chart and lost. Oh, and did we mention your lab results? Of course, records from your hospital stay are separate from records in your doctor's office. And getting a doctor's OK for a prescription refill requires a fax from the pharmacy to the doctor and another fax from the doctor to the pharmacy.

In the past, I (Barry) was an EDP auditor for a life and health insurance company, and I can assure you that insurance claims paperwork was and is inefficient.

To add to your concerns, none of the above information is of any use if, God forbid, you are in a serious traffic accident away from your home town. The Emergency Medical Technician (EMT) who treats you at the scene will have no clue as to your blood type, current medications, or allergic reaction to penicillin. This is not a very encouraging prospect.

By contrast, imagine your health information is stored in a SAN. This includes complete text and imaging data. In this scenario, almost every field of information on the documents described above is available for viewing and updating, over the Internet, by practitioners you authorize. All it takes is a robust SAN and the appropriate application software. Duplication of information and multiple pieces of paper are eliminated.

To return to the scene of the accident, with a SAN you have a much better chance of surviving. In the SAN-based medical scenario, the EMT takes your vital signs, identifies you, and sends a request for information through a wireless link from his or her helmet to the ambulance, and on to the local hospital. The request is transmitted to a national SAN-based medical data repository.

Your medical data comes to the emergency room doctors at the hospital and to the EMT who's trying to save you. The doctor directs the EMT about initial actions to take, views you through the video camera on the EMT's helmet, and reads your signs through transmitted signals. When you arrive at the emergency room, you get X-rays and a CAT scan. Minutes later, that data is appended to your electronic file. If you're in really bad shape, it will be shared electronically with remotely located trauma specialists.

Will all this cost a great deal more? Perhaps not. Mass storage is a very cost-effective way to consolidate information and eliminate unnecessary paper pushing. There may be enough savings to extend health care to many who do not currently have it available to them.

10.6.5 Science

Clearly, it takes a lot of computing power and a lot of mass storage to make gains in some branches of science. The SAN will permit this to happen.

As mentioned at the beginning of this chapter, sequencing the human genome has advanced considerably, using supercomputers and a lot of stored data—over 80 TB and growing. We would expect that any gene research would require storage of immense amounts of data.

Project Phoenix is the successor to the NASA SETI (Search for Extraterrestrial Intelligence) program that was cancelled by Congress in 1993. It tries to find extraterrestrial civilizations by listening for radio signals that are either being deliberately or inadvertently transmitted from another planet. According to the project's Web page, millions of radio channels are simultaneously monitored. Most of the "listening" is done by computers, and two billion channels are examined for each target star. It follows that a SAN would overcome storage limitations, and supercomputers would allow candidate signals to be found and evaluated faster. Unfortunately, the project is privately funded, and the necessary computing and SAN storage resources might be out of the project's reach.

It's apparent that better tools enable more efficient scientific achievement. From examining the origins of the universe to investigating sub-atomic particles, scientific research collects a lot of data. Research will advance faster with SAN technology to store that data.

10.6.6 Music

I (Barry) was told years ago by the advertising manager of a Hollywood radio station that some day people would never need to own physical music recordings (they were LPs in those days, but the reasoning extends to cassette tapes, CDs, and DVDs). Say what? Why should they, the executive told me, when they could get all the music they wanted, whenever they wanted it, just by dialing a telephone? At the time, I was startled by this crazy concept, but as it turns out, she was absolutely right. She had inadvertently predicted MP3.

As this book goes to press, there is a raging controversy over fair payment of royalties for downloaded intellectual properties, rock music in particular. If we can work this out, we stand at the threshold of a new era for audio art: delivering more music to more people than any artist has ever dreamed of.

It makes sense. At this moment, online bookstores sell music CDs—plastic disks in plastic boxes. They are missing the point; they should be selling music.

Given that the nominal capacity of a CD is 650 MB of data, it would take a SAN with only 650 TB of storage to deliver the content of one million CDs. The Internet would be the delivery mechanism, and various consumer music storage devices would be the target storage devices. Yes, we're doing some of this now, but the key difference is the one million CDs. That takes a SAN.

10.6.7 The Library of Everything

What if you could put all the information about something in one library? How about all the information about everything? The library wouldn't need to be near you if you could access it electronically. It need not even be one library, if a number of remotely located libraries worked in concert. What a concept!

To put it another way, isn't it about time all the books were in a SAN-based library? The operative word here is "all."

There have been some very successful experiments with delivering books in HTML or PDF format over the Internet. For example, to read *Huckleberry Finn* or de Tocqueville's *Democracy in America*, head for the University of Virginia Web site. No fuss, no muss, no tax, no tips. It's fast and free.

Unfortunately, putting books on the World Wide Web is all too frequently a labor of love, or part of the vision of a university library. What is not a reality yet is a complete and codified body of learning. But with SANs, it can happen.

We could look to the public libraries and colleges to do this task. The trouble is that at the moment public and university libraries are not among the best-funded institutions in our country. It's a big task, but SAN technology could handle it—if there is the will to pay for it.

A good start in organizing information is the Dewey Decimal Classification System and the ubiquitous card catalog. The system was conceived by Melvil Dewey in 1873 and was first published in 1876.

According to the Online Computer Library Center (OCLC), the Dewey Decimal Classification System is the most widely used library classification system in the world. It is used in more than 135 countries and has been translated into over 30 languages. In the United States, 95% of all public and school libraries, 25% of all college and university libraries, and 20% of special libraries use the DDCS.

Companies like Data Research Associates (DRA) of St. Louis, MO, and Monterey, CA, provide library systems software, including the card catalog component. The next step is for card catalog lookups to display links to all the found books. Those books will be stored on a number of SANs.

The conventional "bricks and mortar" library is not obsolete. People will always want to enjoy the quiet, page through paper books, and use the free Internet connections available there. And we'll still need the wise librarian, because a satisfactory electronic metaphor for that person still has not been developed.

10.7 The Final Word

The SAN is a powerful amalgamation of rapidly evolving technologies: processors, interconnect strategies, storage devices. The evolution is obviously moving in the direction of greater speed, greater capacity, and more complex interconnections.

The power of the SAN derives not only from performance increases in its individual components, but, significantly, from a theoretically limitless ability to add and mix components. Add to that the power of a world of wired and wireless Internet connections. Those connections will be made by billions of people hungry for information.

Information is our most valuable "unnatural" resource. It can make civilizations, bring down dictators, enhance the prosperity of peoples, and, potentially promote peace.

The SAN is a technology that will change the world. And the world will change to the extent that people are committed to changing it. How will the world change because of the SAN? That's up to you, so this chapter is really one you'll have to finish yourself.

Glossary

8B/10B Encoding An encoding scheme, developed by IBM, that encodes 8-bit bytes into 10-bit transmission characters.

Accelis A Linear Tape-Open (LTO) tape format. Accelis tapes are dual-reel tapes with a capacity of up to 50 GB (assuming 2:1 compression). Accelis tapes trade capacity for speed, in contrast to Ultrium tapes.

Adapter A printed circuit assembly that transmits data (I/Os) between the host system's internal bus and the external Fibre Channel link and vice versa. Also called an I/O adapter, host adapter, host bus adapter (HBA), or FC adapter.

Address The logical location of a peripheral device, node, or any other unit or component in a network. The formatted number specifying a network location. See *SCSI address* and *FC-AL address*.

AL_PA Arbitrated Loop Physical Address.

Arbitrated Loop Fibre Channel Arbitrated Loop or FC-AL.

Arbitrated Loop Physical Address The lower eight bits of the 24-bit native address identifier, the N_Port ID. 126 of the 256 possible values are used for addressing devices on a loop.

Arbitration A process where devices on a Fibre Channel Arbitrated Loop contend for and gain temporary, exclusive access to loop resources.

Area The second byte of the N_Port Identifier.

Asynchronous Event Detection (HP's Event Monitoring Service)   The ability to detect an event at the time it occurs. When an event occurs, the monitor is immediately aware of it. This method provides quicker notification than polling.

ATM   Asynchronous Transfer Mode. A transport mechanism used in wide area networks.

Attenuation   The difference (loss) between transmitted and received power, due to the transmission loss through equipment lines or other communications devices. Fiber optic cable is expected to have minimum attenuation, although excessive bends or crimps in the medium can produce signal loss.

Auto Path XP   An optional software package for the XP256 disk array. It provides open (UNIX) and Windows NT systems with failover and load balancing capabilities over multiple paths from the server to the disk array.

Bandwidth   The range of frequencies that can pass over a given circuit. Generally, the greater the bandwidth, the more information that can be sent through the circuit in a given amount of time. In data storage and data communications, bandwidth is usually expressed in terms of the amount of information sent over time, such as Mbps or Gbps.

Baud   The encoded bit rate per second. A measure of transmission speed.

Bridge   A device used to connect a SCSI device to a Fibre Channel network. For example, the HP A3308A Fibre Channel/SCSI 4/2 Bridge can connect four SCSI devices to the SAN over two Fibre Channel paths.

Business Copy XP   An optional software package used with the XP256 disk array. It allows for rapid data copies between source and target volumes. Data copies are used in testing, development, data protection, and disaster recovery scenarios.

Cascaded FC_AL Hubs   One FC-AL hub connected to another FC-AL hub to increase distance or the number of ports in an arbitrated loop. Cascaded hubs allow distances up to 10 kilometers between hubs.

Class (of Service)   The types of services provided by the Fibre Channel topology and used by the communicating port. Class 1 is connection-oriented with acknowledged delivery. Class 2 is connectionless with acknowledged delivery. Class 3 (datagram service) is connectionless, with unacknowledged delivery. The device drivers determine if data is not received and needs to be retransmitted. Class 3 service is also known as "send and pray" service. Class 4 service is "fractional service." It is connection-oriented and uses a fraction of the bandwidth of the link between two ports for communication between the ports. Class 6 service is known as unidirectional dedicated connection service. It is connection-oriented and provides (as the name indicates) dedicated unidirectional connections. Classes 4 and 6 are defined, but are not widely implemented.

Continuous Access XP   An optional software package used with the XP256 disk array. It allows for rapid data copies between source and target volumes, and is used for data protection and backups. Continuous Access copies may be made between volumes in the same disk array or between disk arrays that are remote from one another. It is frequently used in disaster recovery configurations.

Custom Volume Size   An optional software package used with the XP256 disk array. It permits the creation of LUNs smaller than the size of the physical disk, to improve performance and efficient use of space.

DAT   Digital Audio Tape. A family of small format (4 mm) helical scan tapes and tape drives, originally developed for recording audio. DDS tapes derive from the form factor, and are more widely used for recording data.

DDS   Digital Data System. A family of 4 mm helical scan tapes and tape drives, based on DAT technology. DDS tapes have evolved through several generations and are now at DDS-4. DAT tapes are less reliable and should not be used in DDS drives. Later DDS tapes use the Media Recognition System (MRS), indicated by metal markers on the tape, to tell a tape drive what generation of tape is being used. DDS-4 tapes hold 40 GB, assuming 2:1 compression. DDS tape is usually used to back up a single server or NAS device.

Default Monitoring Requests   The default monitoring configuration created when the EMS Hardware Monitors are installed. The default requests ensure that a complete level of protection is automatically provided for all supported hardware resources.

Disparity   A property of 8B/10B encoded bytes. A byte has negative disparity if there are more binary ones in the byte than binary zeroes, and positive disparity if there are more zeroes than ones. A byte has neutral disparity when the number of binary ones equals the number of binary zeroes.

DLT   Digital Linear Tape. A tape technology widely used in backups. Current versions of DLT have a capacity of up to 80 GB, assuming 2:1 compression. DLT tapes are used in single mechanisms and in tape libraries storing from 10 to 1000 DLT cartridges.

Domain   The most significant byte in the N_Port Identifier for an FC device. It is not used in the FC-SCSI hardware path ID. It is required to be the same for all SCSI targets logically connected to an FC adapter.

E_Port   A Fibre Channel switch expansion port, used to link Fibre Channel switches.

EMS   Event Monitoring Service.

ESCON   Enterprise Systems Connection Architecture, an IBM technology used primarily for connecting mainframes to storage devices over fiber optic cable.

Event Monitoring Service   The application framework used for monitoring system resources on servers running HP-UX 10.20 and 11.0. Hardware monitoring uses the EMS framework for reporting events and creating PSM monitoring requests. A collection of EMS system monitors are available at additional cost and are not included with the hardware monitoring software.

Event Severity Level   An Event Monitoring Service term. Each event that occurs within the hardware is assigned a severity level, which reflects the impact the event may have on system operation. The severity levels provide the mechanism for directing event notification. For example, you may choose a notification method for critical events that will alert you immediately to their occurrence, and direct less important events to a log file for examination at your convenience. Also, when used with MC/ServiceGuard to determine failover criteria, severe and critical events cause failover.

F_Port   An F_Port on a Fibre Channel switch connects to an N_Port on a device.

FL_Port   An FL_Port on a Fibre Channel switch connects to an arbitrated loop.

Fabric   A crosspoint switched network, which is one of three Fibre Channel topologies. A fabric consists of one or more fabric elements, which are switches responsible for frame routing. The fabric structure is transparent to the devices connected to it and relieves them of the responsibility for station management.

Fabric Switch   A device that enables the Fibre Channel fabric topology. A core building block of the Storage Area Network.

FC-AL   Fibre Channel Arbitrated Loop.

FC-AL Address   The eight-bit device address on a private Fibre Channel Arbitrated Loop. Addresses are assigned automatically on initialization.

FC-AL Device   A device that can be used in a Fibre Channel Arbitrated Loop. It has one or more NL_Ports.

FC-AL Port   The port on an FC-AL hub that provides connection between the FC-AL adapter and the FC-AL link. Hewlett-Packard FC-AL hubs are 10-port hubs.

FC-SCSI Hardware Path   A list of values, presented by the HP-UX ioscan command, showing the physical hardware path of the host to a target device. The format is:

Fiber   Fiber optic cable.

Fiber Optic Cable   A cable made from thin strands of dielectric material, such as glass, through which data in the form of light pulses is transmitted by laser or LED. Fiber optic cable is used for high-speed transmission over medium to long distances.

Fiber Optics   A technology that uses light as an information carrier. Fiber optic cables are a direct replacement for conventional coaxial cable and wire pairs. The glass-based transmission medium occupies less physical volume for an equivalent transmission capacity, and the fibers are immune to electrical interference.

Fibre   A generic Fibre Channel term used to describe all transmission media specified in the Fibre Channel Physical Layer standard (FC-PH), including optical fiber, copper twisted pair, and copper coaxial cable.

Fibre Channel   Logically, Fibre Channel is a bidirectional, full-duplex, point-to-point, serial data channel structured for high performance capability. Physically, Fibre Channel interconnects devices, such as host systems and servers, FC hubs and disk arrays, through ports, called N_Ports, in one of three topologies: a point-to-point link, an arbitrated loop, or a crosspoint switched network (also called a fabric). Fibre Channel can interconnect two devices in a point-to-point topology, from two to 126 devices in an arbitrated loop, and over 14 million devices in a fabric.

Fibre Channel is a generalized transport mechanism. It has no protocol or native I/O command set, but can transport any existing protocol, such as

SCSI, in frames. Fibre Channel is capable of operating at speeds of 100 MBps (full speed), 50 MBps (half speed), 25 MBps (quarter speed), or 12.5 MBps (eighth speed), over distances of up to 100 m over copper media or up to 10 km over fiber optic cable.

Fibre Channel Arbitrated Loop (FC-AL)   One of three Fibre Channel topologies, in which two to 126 ports can be interconnected serially in a single loop circuit. Access to the FC-AL is controlled by an arbitration scheme. The FC-AL topology supports all classes of service and guarantees in-order delivery of frames.

Fibre Channel Arbitrated Loop Hub   A full-duplex, 1 Gbps intelligent interconnection device, used in an FC-AL topology to create a loop. A maximum of ten devices can be connected to each FC-AL hub.

Fibre Channel Protocol for SCSI (FCP)   A high-level Fibre Channel mapping layer (FC-4) that uses lower-level Fibre Channel services (FC-PH) to transmit SCSI command, data, and status information between a SCSI initiator and a SCSI target across the Fibre Channel link using Fibre Channel frame and sequence formats.

Frame   A collection of bits that contain both control information and data; the basic unit of transmission on a network. Control information is carried in the frame with the data to provide for functions such as addressing, sequencing, flow control, and error control to the respective protocol levels. It can be of fixed or variable length.

The smallest, indivisible unit of data transfer used by Fibre Channel. Frame size depends on the hardware implementation and is independent of the application software. Frames begin with a 4-byte Start of Frame (SOF), end with a 4-byte End of Frame (EOF), include a 24-byte frame header and a 4-byte Cyclic Redundancy Check (CRC), and can carry a variable data payload from 0 to 2112 bytes, the first 64 of which can be used for optional headers.

G_Port   A Fibre Channel switch port that can function either as an E_Port or as an F_Port.

GBIC   Gigabit Interface Converter.

GBps   Gigabytes per second.

Gbps   Gigabits per second.

Gigabit Interface Converter   A removable component of Fibre Channel host
    bus adapters that manages the functions of the FC-0 layer, which are the
    physical characteristics of the media and interface. HBAs have either a
    GBIC or a GLM.

Gigabit Link Module   A physical component that manages the functions of
    the FC-0 layer, which are the physical characteristics of the media and
    interface, including driver, transceivers, connectors, and cables. Also
    referred to as a Physical Link Module (PLM).

GLM   Gigabit Link Module.

HA   High Availability.

Hardware Event Monitor   An Event Monitoring Service monitor daemon
    that gathers information about the operational status of hardware resources.
    Each monitor is responsible for watching a specific group or type of
    hardware resources. For example, the tape monitor handles all tape devices
    on the system. The monitor may use polling or asynchronous event
    detection for tracking events. Unlike a status monitor, an event monitor
    does not "remember" the occurrence of an event. It simply detects and
    reports the event. An event can be converted into a more permanent status
    condition using the Peripheral Status Monitor.

Hardware Event   An Event Monitoring Service term for any unusual or
    notable activity experienced by a hardware resource (for example, a disk
    drive that is not responding, or a tape drive that does not have a tape
    loaded). When any such activity occurs, the occurrence is reported as an
    event to the event monitor.

Hardware Resource   An Event Monitoring Service term for a hardware
    device used in system operation. Resources supported by hardware

monitoring include mass storage devices such as disks and tapes, connectivity devices such as hubs and multiplexers, and device adapters.

HBA   Host Bus Adapter.

High Availability   A term applied to some disk arrays and clustered server configurations. High availability implies that the device can sense, report, and recover from some hardware failures. High availability components include redundant power supplies, fans, system processors (SPs), and RAID-enabled disk drives.

HIPPI   High Performance Parallel Interface. A high-speed interface.

Host   A processor using a disk array for data storage and retrieval.

Host Bus Adapter (HBA)   A printed circuit assembly which transmits data between the host system's internal bus and the external Fibre Channel link and vice versa.

Hub   A device used to connect several nodes in a network. A hub is a concentration point for data and repeats data from one node to all other connected nodes.

Initiator   In SCSI, the server that initiates an exchange with a disk or tape. The Fibre Channel equivalent term is originator.

ioscan   An HP-UX command used to identify devices on a bus and determine their states.

IT   Information Technology. An all-encompassing term for the information processing profession and work done with computers and data. The current name for the department formerly known as the MIS (Management Information Systems) Department, and before that, the Data Processing Department. Also the term for a course of study in colleges and universities.

JBOD   Just a Bunch of Disks. A collection of disk drives in an enclosure, which may or may not have high availability characteristics.

LAN   Local Area Network.

Light Emitting Diode (LED)   A small light on a device that is often used to provide status information. LNK, LINK, ERR, STATUS, ACT, and POWER are typical LED labels.

Link   In Fibre Channel, two unidirectional fiber cables, transmitting in opposite directions, and their associated transmitters and receivers. The link is the connection between nodes in a topology. Comparable to a bus in SCSI.

LIP   Loop Initialization Primitive. The sequence that allows for discovery of ports on the loop.

Logical Unit Size Expansion   An optional software package used with the XP256 disk array. It permits the creation of expanded LUNs, larger than the size of the physical disk.

Longwave   Lasers or LEDs that emit light with wavelengths around 1300 nm. Longwave lasers are used for long Fibre Channel links, from approximately 700 to 10,000 meters. They are typically used with single-mode 9 micron fiber optic cable.

Longwave Hub   A Fibre Channel Arbitrated Loop hub employing long wave lasers and 9 micron single mode fiber optic cable.

Loop Address   The unique ID of a node in Fibre Channel loop topology, sometimes referred to as a Loop ID.

Loop Port (L_Port)   An N_Port or F_Port that supports arbitrated loop functions associated with arbitrated loop topology.

LTO   Linear Tape-Open. A new tape technology, specifying improved capacity and transfer rates over existing DDS and DLT technologies.

LUN   Logical Unit Number, or logical unit. A physical disk drive (or portion of it) that can be addressed as an entity. An HP-UX hardware path might show 8/12.8.0.255.0.1.0, where the final zero represents LUN 0. For practical purposes, a drive (such as G:\ or I:\) on a Windows NT system. The XP256 disk array may have LUNs smaller than a disk, using the

Custom Volume Size feature, or LUNs spanning disks, using the Logical Unit Size Expansion feature.

Mbps   Megabits per second.

MBps   Megabytes per second.

MC/ServiceGuard   Hewlett-Packard's application for creating and managing high availability clusters of HP 9000 Series 800 computers. A high availability computer system allows application services to continue in spite of a hardware or software failure. Hardware monitoring integrates with MC/ServiceGuard to detect and report hardware problems, allowing MC/ServiceGuard to take action to maintain system availability.

Monitoring Request   Event Monitoring Service settings that define how events for a specific monitor are handled by EMS. A monitoring request identifies the severity levels of interest and the type of notification method to use when an event occurs. A monitoring request is applied to each hardware device (or instance) supported by the monitor. Monitoring requests are created for hardware events using the Hardware Monitoring Request Manager. You create monitoring requests for changes in hardware status using the EMS GUI.

N_Port   Node port. A hardware entity that performs data communication over the Fibre Channel link. It is identifiable by a unique World Wide Name (WWN). It can act as an originator or a responder.

N_Port Identifier   A unique 24-bit address by which an N_Port is known. The address consists of a Domain (most significant byte), an Area, and a Port, each 1 byte long. The N_Port identifier is used in the Source Identifier (S_ID) and Destination Identifier (D_ID) fields of a Fibre Channel frame.

NAS   Network Attached Storage.

Non-OFC   A low-intensity laser transceiver whose output does not require OFC to turn off the laser when there is a disconnect.

Node   The hardware device that allows for the transmission of data within a network. A node contains one or more ports.

OFC   Open Fibre Control. A safety feature used to prohibit laser light from functioning when there is a break or disconnect in a fiber cable. This is used with high-intensity lasers.

OC-3   A wide area network leased line service connection, running at a speed of up to 155 Mbps.

OC-12   A wide area network leased line service connection, running at a speed of up to 622 Mbps.

OLTP   Online Transaction Processing.

Originator   The Fibre Channel N_Port responsible for starting an exchange. Fibre Channel term for a SCSI initiator.

Ordered Set   A transmission word beginning with a K28.5 special character. Ordered sets permit special control functions to be embedded in the bit stream, including frame delimiter, primitive signals, and primitive sequences.

Performance Manager XP   An optional software package used with the XP256 disk array. Its purpose is to monitor disk array performance, display real time status, capture the information in logs, and display a variety of performance graphs. The user may also make adjustments to settings on a real time or scheduled basis.

Peripheral Status Monitor (PSM)   Part of the Event Monitoring Service, the PSM is included with the hardware event monitors. It is a monitor daemon that acts as a hardware status monitor by converting events to changes in hardware resource status. This provides compatibility with MC/ServiceGuard, which uses changes in status to manage cluster resources. The PSM is also used to create hardware status monitoring requests through the EMS GUI.

Point-to-point   One of three Fibre Channel topologies. With the point-to-point topology, two devices are directly connected by a link with no fabric, loop, or switching elements present.

Polling   In event monitoring, the process of connecting to a hardware resource at regular intervals to determine its status. Any events that occur between polling intervals will not be detected until the next poll. If the event monitor supports asynchronous event monitoring, events will be reported immediately.

Port   The hardware entity that connects a device to a Fibre Channel topology. A device can contain one or more ports.

Primitive Sequence   A set of three identical ordered sets for link control. These are used for notification of link failures and loss of synchronization.

Primitive Signal   Used for buffer-to-buffer flow control, or for idle primitives. Idles are words that fill the space between frames. In Fibre Channel, the transmitter must continuously send something over the media. This helps preserve bit, byte, and word synchronization, and permits faster communication.

Private Loop   A private loop is enclosed and known only to itself. A common example configuration uses FC-AL for Fibre Channel Mass Storage, and the processor node only has one Fibre Channel host bus adapter (HBA).

Protocol   A formal set of rules governing the format, timing, sequencing, and error control of exchanged messages on a data network. It may also include facilities for managing a communications link and/or contention resolution. A protocol may be oriented toward data transfer over an interface, between two logical units directly connected, or on an end-to-end basis between two end users over a large and complex network. Both hardware protocols and software protocols can be defined.

Public Loop   A public loop extends the reach of the loop topology by attaching the loop to a fabric. Public loops are a way to leverage the cost of one switched connection over many devices in a loop.

RAID   Redundant Array of Independent Disks. A method of configuring multiple disk modules into a logical disk unit, which appears to the host system as a single, contiguous disk module.

RAID-0   A disk configuration with three or more disk modules bound as striped disks. The disk array reads and writes file information to more than one disk at a time. RAID-0 offers enhanced performance by using simultaneous I/O to different modules, but does not intrinsically offer high availability. For high availability, the striped disks can be software mirrored.

RAID-1   A disk configuration with even numbers of mirrored disk modules.

RAID-1/0   A disk configuration in which four, six, eight, ten, twelve, fourteen, or sixteen disk modules are bound as a mirrored RAID-0 group. The disk modules are mirrored such that one half the disk modules contain user data and the other half contain a disk-by-disk copy of the user data. A RAID-1/0 group combines the speed advantage of RAID-0 with the redundancy advantage of mirroring.

RAID-3   A disk configuration consisting of exactly five disk modules, each on a separate internal single-ended SCSI-2 bus. RAID-3 uses disk striping and a dedicated parity disk, but not hardware mirroring.

RAID-5   A disk configuration in which from three to sixteen disk modules use disk striping, with high availability provided by parity information distributed on each disk module. The ideal number of disk modules in a RAID-5 group is five.

RAIL   Random Array of Independent Libraries.

Resource Instance   An Event Monitoring Service term for a specific hardware device. The resource instance is the last element of the resource path and is typically the hardware path to the resource (for example, 10_12_5.0.0), but it may also be a product ID as in the case of AutoRAID disk arrays. There may be multiple resource instances for a monitor, each one representing a unique hardware device for which the monitor is responsible.

Resource Path (EMS)   Hardware event monitors are organized into classes (and subclasses) for creating monitoring requests. These classes identify a unique path to each hardware resource supported by the monitor. Two similar resource paths exist for each hardware resource: an event path used for creating event monitoring requests, and a status path used for creating PSM monitoring requests.

Responder   The logical function in an N_Port responsible for supporting the exchange initiated by the originator in another N_Port. A Fibre Channel term for a SCSI target.

SAN   Storage Area Network.

SCSI-3   Ultra3 SCSI. A type of SCSI using a 16 data-bit wide bus, and which transfers data at a maximum of 160 MB per second. Hewlett-Packard has chosen to support the SCSI-3 protocol over Fibre Channel for its mass storage environment.

SCSI   Small Computer System Interface. An industry standard for connecting peripheral devices to a processor.

SCSI Address   A fast/wide SCSI adapter supports up to 16 devices, including itself. Each device has a unique SCSI address. The SCSI address of a device dictates the devices's priority when arbitrating for the SCSI bus. SCSI address "7" has the highest priority. The next highest priority address is "6" followed by 5, 4, 3, 2, 1, 0, 15, 14, 13, 12, 11, 10, 9, and 8. The SCSI adapter is factory set to address "7."

A narrow SCSI adapter supports up to eight devices, including itself. SCSI address "7" has the highest priority followed by 6, 5, 4, 3, 2, 1, and 0.

SCSI Bus   The conduit for transferring SCSI data between servers and SCSI devices through SCSI host bus adapters and SCSI ports.

SCSI Port   An opening at the back of a SCSI device providing connection between the SCSI adapter and the SCSI bus. SCSI connectors come in 50-pin or 68-pin configurations.

Shortwave   Lasers or LEDs that emit light with wavelengths of 780 nm or 850 nm. Shortwave lasers are used for Fibre Channel links up to approximately 500 meters long, over multimode fiber. The preferred fiber core size is 50 microns. A 62.5 micron core size is also supported for compatibility with existing FDDI installations.

Shortwave Hub   A Fibre Channel Arbitrated Loop hub employing shortwave lasers and 50 or 62.5 micron multimode fiber optic cable.

Source Volume   The volume or LUN containing data to be copied to a target volume in Continuous Access or Business Copy operations on an XP256 disk array.

SNMP   Simple Network Management Protocol.

SP   Storage Processor.

Storage Area Network   An arrangement of storage devices, connected in a loop or fabric, using Fibre Channel.

Storage Processor   A printed-circuit board with memory modules that controls the disk modules in the storage system chassis. The SP runs Grid Manager, which is used to bind and unbind logical disk units, set up disk array caching, observe array status, and view the SP event log. The SP in a disk array divides the multiplexed SCSI-2 bus traffic from the host into five internal, single-ended, SCSI-2 buses (identified by the letters A, B, C, D, and E). Each internal SCSI-2 bus supports multiple logical units (LUNs).

Storage Node Manager   A SAN management software application made by Hewlett-Packard.

Striping   Short for data striping. (1) Used to achieve higher bandwidth, by allowing multiple links simultaneously and transmitting a single information unit across multiple links employing multiple N_Ports in parallel. Sometimes called port aggregation. (2) A mapping technique in which fixed-size consecutive ranges of virtual disk data addresses are mapped to successive array members in a cyclic pattern. RAID Level 0 or RAID 0.

Switch   For the purposes of SANs, a fabric switch. A Fibre Channel connection device that provides multiple, simultaneous full-bandwidth connections between devices.

T-1 A wide area network leased line service connection, running at a speed of up to 1.544 Mbps.

T-3 A wide area network leased line service connection, running at a speed of up to 45 Mbps.

Tape Library A device containing one or more tape drives and a varying number of tapes. Tapes are moved from library slots to the drives under robot control. A small tape library might have one drive and ten slots for tapes. The largest HP tape library has 20 drives and 700 slots for tapes. Tape libraries are an essential component of backup and restore operations in large SANs.

Target In SCSI, the disk or tape device responding to an initiator. The Fibre Channel equivalent term is responder.

Target ID (TID) The SCSI bus address of a controller or target device.

Target Volume The volume or LUN receiving data from a source volume, using Continuous Access or Business Copy on an XP256 disk array.

Topology The physical arrangement of devices on a network.

Ultrium A Linear Tape-Open (LTO) tape format. First-generation Ultrium tapes currently have a capacity of up to 200 GB with 400 GB, 600 GB, and 1.6 TB on the generational "roadmap" (assuming 2:1 compression).

WAN Wide Area Network.

World Wide Name A 64-bit identifier assigned to a device. It uniquely identifies the device.

Zoning Limiting access by servers to LUNs, based on a device's World Wide Name. Implemented by HP's Secure LUN software.

Bibliography

General References

1. Bellamy, Edward. *Looking Backward*. Dover Publications, 1996. ISBN 0486290387.

2. Berners-Lee, Tim and Fischetti, Mark. *Weaving the Web: The Original Design and Ultimate Destiny of the World Wide Web by Its Inventor*. Harper, San Francisco, CA, 1999. ISBN 0062515861.

3. Clark, Tom. *Designing Storage Area Networks*. Addison-Wesley Longman, Reading, MA, 1999. ISBN 0201615843.

4. Dedek, Jan and Stephens, Gary. *What is FIBRE CHANNEL?* ANCOT Corporation, Menlo Park, CA, 1996. ISBN 0963743953.

5. Dertouzos, Michael. *What Will Be: How the New World of Information Will Change Our Lives*. Harper Business, 1998. ISBN 0062515403.

6. Fibre Channel Association. *Fibre Channel: Connection to the Future*. Austin, TX, 1994. ISBN 1878707191.

7. *INFOSTOR 3,* Nos. 6-12 (June-December 1999).

8. *INFOSTOR 4,* Nos. 1-5 (January-May 2000).

9. Musashi, Miyamoto. *The Book of Five Rings: The Real Art of Japanese Management*. Bantam Books, 1982. ISBN 055322509X.

10. Myers, P.V.N. *A General History*. Ginn & Company, Boston, 1897.

11. Stephens, Gary and Dedek, Jan. *FIBRE CHANNEL The Basics*. ANCOT Corporation, Menlo Park, CA, 1997. ISBN 0963743937.

12. Toffler, Alvin. *Future Shock*. Bantam Books, 1971. ISBN 0553277375.

13. Toffler, Alvin. *The Third Wave: The Classic Study of Tomorrow*. Bantam Books, 1981. ISBN 0553246984.

Resources on the World Wide Web

1.   www.aspindustry.org (Application Service Providers Industry Consortium)

2.   www.brocade.com (Brocade Communications Systems)

3.   www.enterprisestorage.hp.com (Hewlett-Packard Company)

4.   www.fibrechannel.com (Fibre Channel Industry Association)

5.   www.ibm.com (International Business Machines Corporation)

6.   www.infostor.com (*INFOSTOR:* News and Information for Enterprise Storage Professionals)

7.   www.iol.unh.edu/consortiums/ (Fibre Channel Consortium of the University of New Hampshire)

8.   www.lto-technology.com (Linear Tape-Open Organization)

9.   www.oclc.org (Online Computer Library Center)

10. www.searchstorage.com (search engine)

11. www.snia.org (Storage Networking Industry Association)

12. www.storagesearch.com (search engine)

13. www.virginia.edu (University of Virginia)

14. http://dir.yahoo.com/Business_and_Economy/Business_to_Business/
Computers/Communications_and_Networking/
Storage_Area_Networks__SANs_/ (Yahoo!'s list of SAN companies)

15. http://members.xoom.com/_XMCM/methomas/colossal.htm
(Colossal Storage)

Hewlett-Packard Product Documents

1. *Hewlett-Packard A5223A Gigabit Fibre Channel Switch Service and User's Guide.* Hewlett-Packard Company, 1999.

2. *Hewlett-Packard Fibre Channel Arbitrated Loop Hub.* Hewlett-Packard Company, 1997.

3. *Hewlett-Packard Fibre Channel Mass Storage Adapters Service and User Manual.* Hewlett-Packard Company, 2000.

4. *Hewlett-Packard Fibre Channel SCSI Multiplexer.* Hewlett-Packard Company, 1997.

5. *Hewlett-Packard High Availability Fibre Channel Disk Array User's Guide.* Hewlett-Packard Company, 1997.

6. *Hewlett-Packard SureStore E Fibre Channel Manager 3.1 User's Manual.* Hewlett-Packard Company, 2000.

Index

Heterogeneous servers 9
High availability 205, 271
HIPPI 48, 271
History of storage 23
Holographic mass storage 247
Host 271
Host Bus Adapter 271
HP SAN products 183
HP SureStore E Disk Array XP256
     210
HP's Fibre Channel chips 184
HPFC-5100 185, 186
Hub 84, 271
     active 84
     cabling examples 202
     cascaded 202
     features 198
     incorrect cabling 203
     longwave 199, 272
     passive 84
     shortwave 199
     topology 200

I

IBM 246
Idle state 79
IEEE 802.2 48
Information Unit (IU) 71
Initiator 271
Intelligent storage 244
Internet 244
ioscan 271
IP 48
IPI 48
IT 271

J

JBOD 34, 271
Job opportunities 251

K

K28.5 special character 64

L

L10 hub 199
LAN 31, 271
LED 272
Libraries and the SAN 259
Light Emitting Diode 272
Linear Tape-Open 154, 272
Link Control Facility (LCF) 59
LIP (Loop Initialization Primitive)
     272
Logical Unit Size Expansion 272
Longwave 61, 272
Longwave hub 199, 272
Loop 52
     address 272
     FC-AL private loop 73
     initialization 76
     LIP 76
     Loop Port Enable (LPE) 76
     LPB 76
     LPE 76
     monitoring state 79
     port bypass 76
     private loop 73
     public loop 74
     states 78
     types of 73
Loop Port (L_Port) 272
Loop Port Bypass (LPB) 76

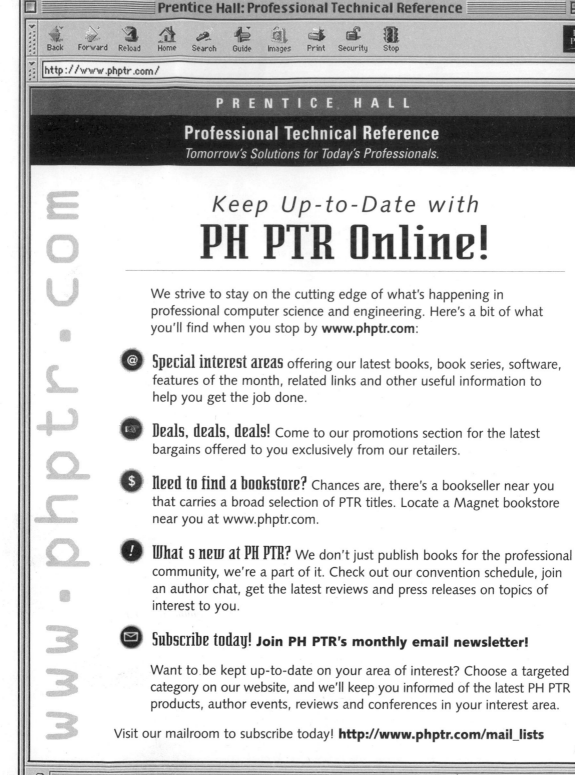